THE EMERALD ROSE

THE EMERALD ROSE

A Courtroom Novel

David Crump

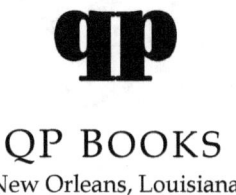

QP BOOKS

New Orleans, Louisiana

Published in 2017 by QP Books, an imprint of Quid Pro Books.

ISBN 978-1-61027-382-4 (paperback)
ISBN 978-1-61027-380-0 (ePUB)

QP BOOKS
Quid Pro, LLC
5860 Citrus Blvd., suite D-101
New Orleans, Louisiana 70123
www.qpbooks.com

This is a work of fiction. The characters, names, events, dialogue and circumstances are imaginary or are used fictionally. Any resemblance to real persons or actual events is purely coincidental, fictitious or imaginary.

Front cover image adapted from an iStock photograph by contributor "mevans," used by permission.

qp

Cataloging-in-Publication Data

Crump, David.
   The Emerald Rose: A Courtroom Novel / David Crump.
      p. cm.
   ISBN 978-1-61027-382-4 (pbk.)

1. Trials—United States—Fiction. 2. Law Firms—United States—Fiction. I. Title.

PS3540.R3923C2 2017   872' .23.4—dc21
                                                       2017179827
                                                       CIP

Author's Preface

I had the same objectives with this book as I've had with my earlier books. I wanted to write a story that would be fun to read, and also to show the practice of law the way it really is.

Most courtroom dramas don't do this. One bestselling book featured a law firm where the partners would kill you if you tried to quit. I've never heard of a firm where they'd kill you if you got out, although I've known some where the work would all but kill you if you stayed in.

I want my novels to show what lawyers really do. They construct documents, battle puzzles with no answers, and get scared of losing. They file suit papers, and they spend a lot of time in "discovery," which is pretrial questioning. Discovery produces a lot of interesting situations, but writers don't cover it much.

Well, you'll follow these activities in this book. You'll see something real.

But now, it's time to get into our story. Imagine that you're a new attorney at the law firm of Robert Herrick and Associates. You're about to participate in a lawsuit that will rattle one of America's greatest industries from top to bottom. And all you have to do is turn the page.

THE EMERALD ROSE

1

There is an offshore oil platform called Thunder Horse. There is another one called Petronius. And then, there are Mad Dog, Bullwinkle, and Baldpate.

And among the floating platforms, there are Magnolia and Mars, which use "tension leg" designs. They're tethered to the ocean floor, but they float, with pontoons on their legs. And beyond those, there are hundreds of platform designs. In fact, every offshore installation is unique. There are jackup rigs, compliant towers, semisubmersibles, and all kinds of other weird contraptions, manufactured in places like Korea and Finland.

All of these unnatural devices share a dangerous characteristic, which is that fires and leaks can occur. They usually are containable, because oil-production platforms bristle with safety mechanisms, and they have backups, sometimes with triple redundancies. But ultimately, they all depend on human operators, and as a result, offshore platforms are accidents waiting to happen.

And that means that these platforms are also lawsuits waiting to happen.

For example, there was that big, big litigation about one of the most unlucky offshore oil rigs of all . . .

. . . the litigation over the platform called the Emerald Rose, also known as the Deepwater Rose.

The Case of the Deepwater Rose was a battle that took years. It was unusual. And during the trial, the unusual happenings started soon after the jury panel entered the courtroom.

2

S it here, please." The deputy pointed, and the first eight citizens took their places in the jury array.

The potential jurors whispered to each other. "It's the Deepwater Rose case!" But these were stage whispers, loud enough to be heard across the courtroom. "This must be about the Emerald Rose! . . ."

Robert Herrick craned his six-foot-two frame upward to see all of the potential jurors as they filed into the courtroom. His hand began to shake, and he stuffed it into the jacket pocket of his suit.

"It doesn't look like a good jury panel for our side," he whispered to Tom Kennedy, his closest partner. The one he worked with most often.

"No, it doesn't," Tom agreed. "Too many managers and professionals. The kinds of folks who aren't sympathetic to plaintiffs' cases."

Across the courtroom, Jimmy Coleman stared at the panel too. He had been Robert's rival in too many courtroom collisions of the past. He sported a tan suit that stretched tightly across his short, flabby frame. Jimmy wore a picture of unrelenting combat on his face, with eyes so cold and dead that witnesses turned away when he cross-examined them.

"This first potential juror is a grocery store manager." Robert's blue eyes squinted at the man's juror information form. "I bet he's seen a thousand slip-and-fall cases, and to him, they're all bogus. He's not likely to be sympathetic to people killed in an offshore platform accident."

"Second one's a high school teacher," Tom added. "She's heard all the excuses from her students, and she's probably figured out she can't believe anybody's sob stories."

Meanwhile, Jimmy Coleman was nodding and beaming, because this was the kind of panel he liked. The third potential juror happened to be a black man, but he was an orthopedic doctor. A natural defendant's juror. Fourth was an insurance adjuster. Best type of all for the defense, and worst for the plaintiff. A ghoulish grin spread all over Jimmy's cigar-stained teeth.

Judge Pamela Preston smiled at the jury panel. Every judge is a politician, because you have to be political to get to be a judge. "Good morning, ladies and gentlemen. The case now on trial involves a group of plaintiffs who are suing the Emerald Petroleum Company and other defendants, allegedly for wrongful death and personal injuries."

Again, the jury panel buzzed. "See, I told you. It's the case of the Emerald Rose." . . . "It's about the Deepwater Rose disaster."

Robert fiddled with the knot on his tie. A nervous habit. He had selected one with red and blue stripes, because experience had shown that jurors disliked anything that grabbed attention. The stripes were woven into the fabric, because he had also learned that high quality conveyed an impression of competence. Maybe jurors figured that quality meant success, and from that, perhaps they inferred that the lawyer had a good case. A dark chalk-striped suit and a plain white shirt completed his lawyer's uniform.

The judge continued her monotone. Reading words she had said many times. "This is a civil case that will be tried before a jury. . . ."

Robert kept scanning the jury panel, hoping for something friendly.

The defense lawyers sometimes called Robert Herrick "The Baby-Faced Assassin" for his youthful appearance and his ability to beat them in the courtroom. The women jurors usually loved him, with his boyish looks and the shock of dark hair over his forehead. The men usually admired his ability to speak forcefully without notes at the end of a long trial, as well as his capacity to admit weaknesses in his cases without showing weakness.

But this jury panel probably wasn't going to show that kind of admiration. "For every potential juror who might favor the plaintiff,"

Tom whispered, "there are four who look like they'll side with the defense."

Now, the judge was telling jurors not to discuss this case with anyone, including their wives and husbands.

Suddenly, a man in torn overalls stood up on the fourth row. "The fix is in!" He shouted. "It's all a fraud. These people aren't hurt at all."

The judge froze, and so did everyone else.

"Lawyers!" the man screamed. "Both sides are in cahoots. They've got the President and a bunch of crooked senators behind them. Whatever these lawyers say happened, you can be sure it didn't happen!"

Now, Judge Preston reacted. "Bailiff, please remove that individual."

The prospective jurors parted like the Red Sea. The bailiff and a courtroom deputy took the deranged man's arms and led him out, twisting and shouting. He was yelling something about all lawyers being "Foreigners, and they kneel down on those toe-sacks they call prayer rugs."

Robert stood. "I move for a mistrial." Probably the jurors weren't persuaded by this crazy man, but there was no sense in taking the risk.

The judge wasn't buying it. "Is there anyone on the jury panel who will be influenced, even in the slightest, by anything said by this man whom the bailiff has removed?"

She paused. "I didn't see or hear anybody. That's what I expected. You are instructed to disregard anything said by the man who was removed, and I'm sure you can all see why."

The judge turned to the plaintiff's lawyers. "I understand your motion, Mr. Herrick." She smiled, just to signal that nothing unusual was going on. "But no, a mistrial is not needed. Let's proceed."

"It's an omen." Tom shook his head. "This crazy, deranged man is an omen. A bad one. And the jury panel is still terrible. Maybe we should have taken the settlement offer Jimmy Coleman made us, as lousy as it was."

"We couldn't, of course, with our clients so opposed to it." Robert snapped his attention away from the screaming man, back to the present. "And now it's too late. We could try to revive that settlement possibility, but Jimmy's not likely to keep that same amount open—now that he's seen this jury panel."

"Why is it that we always run into this kind of luck?"

"This one started out with bad luck four years ago."

And for an instant, while the judge was continuing her opening instructions to the jurors, Robert Herrick thought back four years. To a time long before this jury panel had formed, and long before the crazy man had shouted.

He though back to the day when survivors of the burning, exploding Emerald Rose Disaster had become his clients. When this crazy man wasn't even a thought.

To the day when he had taken on the Case of the Emerald Rose.

3

Four *years earlier . . .*

The newspaper headline was two inches high, above the fold. "TWENTY-SEVEN DEAD." A full-color photograph taken from a helicopter showed the Emerald Rose blazing spectacularly, with a red-and-yellow methane flame enveloping its broken cranes, while the structure listed at almost a thirty-degree angle.

"This has got to be one of the worst oil patch accidents in America." Robert Herrick sat on a tan leather sofa across from his wife in the living room of their home in River Oaks. The sun curled through the thick plantation shutters and onto the oriental carpet.

"It may not be the worst, but it's bad enough." His wife, Maria Melendes, was an assistant district attorney. "You and I both tend to look at these things in terms of legalisms, like negligence, proximate cause, and damages. But when I look at this incident, it's just the sheer tragedy that I see."

The television screen suddenly showed file footage of the burning platform. Maria turned the sound up.

"Good evening, friends," said the anchor, with a toothpaste-ad smile. "I'm John Moreno, and . . . this . . . is . . . Action News!" He was silhouetted in what television producers call chroma key, with the burning platform behind him. The picture was eerie. It made him look as though his shoulders were on fire.

"The Emerald Rose platform isn't burning anymore." John Moreno's face was somber, now. "But this well has spilled oil by the thousands of barrels into the Gulf of Mexico. Luckily, that oil flow was stopped early on. The dead number twenty-seven, but we are told ominously that there may be more, because the injured include several who are burned critically."

"How did this happen?" was what Robert wanted to know. The television set was about to give him a version of an answer.

"Action News's Andrea Martin is live right now." John Moreno's voice rose expectantly. "She has an expert standing by in Port Arthur, where this rig was serviced. Andrea?"

"That's right, John." The picture shifted to a newswoman who stood beside a man in heavy work clothes gleaming with the blackness of oil, soaking into twill that was John Deere green. "This is Joe Don Emerson here with me, and he's been a safety officer on offshore rigs for more than twenty years."

She pivoted. "Mr. Emerson, what do you think caused this accident?" She pointed the microphone toward him.

"A blowout of some kind. Sudden pressure that throws the drilling mud out and spews natural gas along with the oil."

"Why did it catch on fire?"

"You're not going to like the answer. It usually catches on fire. Almost always. Or it explodes, just the way it did here. In the middle of all of that rushing gas, and with all of that incredible pressure, there's going to be a spark. There's bound to be a little bitty spark. And that's all it takes."

"It's not supposed to happen."

"No. It sure isn't."

"Why did it happen here, Mr. Emerson?"

"That's one of the things we don't know yet. The well includes a stack of mechanisms, really big valves, called 'Blowout Preventers.' In this case, on the sea bed. And obviously, there was a blowout, so the Blowout Preventers didn't prevent the blowout like they were supposed prevent it."

"Well, yes," was Andrea Martin's sage reply.

"And in fact there are several redundancies, and they didn't work either, apparently."

"What kind of redundancies?"

"That means there were several of the same types of things. Annular Blowout Preventers, circling the wellbore to shut it if needed. And Shear Rams, which are supposed to close the pipe. But they didn't."

Emerson-the-expert waved his arms. "Sometimes that happens. Sometimes the conditions are just right and the pressure builds up and nothing can hold it."

"There you have it." She nodded knowingly. "Andrea Martin, Action News, in Port Arthur, where the Emerald Rose platform was serviced."

Robert and Maria stared at the screen. Finally, Robert spoke up. "Well, we don't know much more than we knew before."

"Well, at least now I've heard of a 'Blowout Preventer.'" She shook her head.

"And now you know that it's designed to prevent blowouts. And usually it does."

"So. Somebody was negligent, here."

"Well . . . , I guess. Probably. But we'll have to wait and see what develops."

* * *

It took only three days before the families of the dead and injured came to see Robert Herrick. They came, the first four families, with children in tow and accompanied by the lawyers they had gone to see first.

The office that housed Robert Herrick and Associates was at the top of the Chase Tower. Tallest building in the city. The families and their lawyers gathered in the big conference room, where the green-house-style windows gave a spectacular view to the west. The meanders of Buffalo Bayou were bordered by green, which merged with the oaks and pines of Memorial Park in the far west, just before they blended into the misty horizon.

"I'm proud to become acquainted with you ladies and gentlemen. And your little ones." Robert smiled as he saw children running to slap their hands against the paneled wall and other little ones picking up telephones. "What can I do for you? How can I help?"

"Well, you know a little about it already." Francel Williams was a longtime friend. "It's about the Emerald Rose Disaster. You sounded skeptical on the telephone, Robert, and we hope you won't be, when we ask for that help you just offered."

Robert smiled again, because Francel Williams always made him smile. Francel was a tall black lawyer who always wore his trademark:

a charcoal pinstripe suit with a silver tie. He had been the first black man to become a court of appeals judge many years ago, but he had chafed against the role of a judge because he wanted to be more active. He didn't like sitting and listening. Near the end of his term, he had gone back to practicing law.

Robert shook his head. "Francel, there are plenty of lawyers in this city who know offshore accidents. Who've learned how platforms work and what goes wrong. Honestly, I'm not one of them."

"But this is a big case, Robert, and it needs you." Francel smiled a big smile. "You're the man for it. You're Mister Big Case! And you don't want to miss out on this one."

"You're touching a nerve, Francel. You know I like an adventure. But a big case means big problems if you don't know what you're doing."

Francel laughed. "Back in the old neighborhood—ah, excuse me, let me say 'back in the 'hood,'" and Francel laughed harder at that, because he had said it just for fun, "—we used to say, 'Protestin ain't no good, if it goes against what you already done wanted.' And I know you, my friend. You already done wanted to take on this case."

"I've got more to carry than I can lift with both arms. We've got twenty-six lawyers now, and they're all too busy to pull any of them away from what they're doing. But the biggest problem is, I just don't know the industry. This calls for someone who's really into oil and gas and offshore production."

Francel just smiled a bigger smile.

Another trademark of Francel was his optimism. Robert recalled an occasion when, during trial, the bailiff had to inform Francel that his Uncle George had died. For a moment, the pinstriped lawyer was thunderstruck. "Uncle George was the one who raised me when my daddy passed away!" Then, the bailiff said quietly, "Your Uncle George had a heart attack while he was teaching his calculus class at Huston-Tillotson College, doing what he loved."

And Francel, after swallowing hard, had beamed and said, "What a wonderful thing to happen to Uncle George!"

That was Francel Williams.

And now, with a voice full of enthusiasm, Francel showed his optimism again. "Robert, it's a straight negligence case. You're the best guy in the world for that! Look at these kids. They're kids without daddies. Because of big shots' greed, in a greedy, big-shot industry. Look at these kids!"

At that, Robert just stared at Francel. Tugging at the buttersoft part of his heart, this way, was a low blow.

"And this is a case that needs the best guy in the world," Francel repeated. "You, Robert."

*　*　*

Twenty minutes later, the crowd moved to the elevators, with Robert wishing them good luck and repeating the names of several lawyers with expertise in the area.

Francel hung back. Still optimistic. Still with a big smile. "Just think about it, Robert. The right thing to do will come to you."

4

And you said No?" Maria Melendes was surprised.

"Well, yes."

"Why?"

"I'm too busy already," he told his wife. "And it's not my area of expertise."

"But it involved your friend Francel. And a lot of orphan kids."

"But those kids can be better represented by a lawyer who does offshore stuff. It's really complicated, you know. Do you suppose they do directional drilling out there? And can you frack the well if it's way under the ocean? I have no idea. I would start that race from ten yards back."

"But you've done complicated cases with lots of plaintiffs before, about things you didn't already know well. Against banks. And terrorists. And all kinds of people."

"I know."

"I'm just surprised, is all." Maria smiled.

He stared at her red-auburn Hispanic hair, in pretty ringlets. At her perfect Cuban skin and the rows of teeth she showed in her smile. She was beautiful, and he liked to look at her. Too often, he thought, she disagrees with me.

And many times, he thought . . . she's right.

* * *

"When you turned down that Deepwater Rose Case," said Tom Kennedy, "I almost fell out of my chair."

Tom sat in front of Robert's big mahogany desk on one of the matching chairs. The day was cloudy and full of heavy mist, but through the floor-to-ceiling windows, the greensward of Buffalo Bayou glistened. The city spires sprouted up to the south and west in colors of brown, gray, and white, while the tiny cars, so many floors below, crept along the spaghetti bowl of freeways.

"Why do you say that, Tom?"

"This Emerald Rose case, or Deepwater Rose, it's a case worthy of our best attention. It's big. And you can help a lot of widows and orphans." This was hard for Tom Kennedy to say, because he wanted the firm to represent more banks and insurance companies. The kind of clients who could pay staggering fees in advance. "And it would really help to build this law firm."

"You know why I didn't take the case, Tom. Offshore litigation requires a lot of technical knowledge that we don't have. And everybody here is working on cases where we do have the knowledge."

"Timing, Robert. It's a matter of timing. If we file suit now, the busy times will be in the future, months from now, with the heaviest load coming something after a year. Or more likely, several years. By then, we'll have settled a lot of the inventory of litigation we have now."

"Well, I guess." Robert sounded doubtful.

*　*　*

Donna deCarlo rang him. "It's Francel Williams, on the phone."

Even though he knew Francel was going to rag him around again about taking the Emerald Rose case, Robert smiled. Because Francel always made him smile.

"Hello, Francel."

"Hi, Robert! I'm looking forward to working with you on this Deepwater Rose case. It'll be fun. I mean, fun like we've had in cases like that propane truck case, or the one against that holding company in New York."

Robert laughed. "Why is it that personal injury lawyers talk about every case as giving them a lot of 'fun'? Whenever someone wants me to get into a hornet's nest that I'm trying to avoid, they always tell me how much fun it's going to be."

"Haaa haaa! That's funny!" Francel had a laugh that filled a room, and Robert could visualize him grinning, now, even through the telephone. "What I mean is, I'll be there with you. And Robert, we've always come out with great results together."

"Hmmmmmm."

"I'll tell you what. I'll study up on offshore platforms myself. I'll be the guy who knows everything, like Mister Spock was on *Star Trek*. You remember Mister Spock? You can be like that lazy-ass Captain Kirk, and you won't have to know about oil platforms. You won't have to know squat."

Robert had to laugh.

"Just think about it." Francel's enthusiasm was at least a little contagious. "You'll see that it's a case that you don't want to miss. This is like *Marbury versus Madison*. And nobody wanted to miss that one."

"Hmmmmm."

"Just think about it, Robert."

"All right. All right!"

Suddenly, he paused. He wasn't sure whether he had promised to think about it—or whether he had just told Francel he would do it.

After Francel had hung up, Robert sat there, looking around his office. And smiling. Because Francel always made him smile. As he looked at his domain, he thought about what he saw. His desk was a work of art itself: a big rectangle of polished mahogany. It sat on a priceless oriental carpet, huge and brilliant in every color, with diamonds, squares, and indescribable shapes. The walls were hung with paintings by Picasso, Mondrian, and Wyeth. Geraniums in red and pink, a hundred of them, bloomed beneath the greenhouse windows.

It's comfortable, he thought. But it's all just *stuff*. And, he thought, my life in the law isn't about this stuff; it's about the journey.

He shook his head at how corny that message sounded.

I suppose I told Francel something more than just I'd think about it, he said to himself.

He picked up the phone.

"Donna, please call Tom."

". . . Hey, Tom. If we're going to take on this Emerald Rose Case, we need two lawyers to do some work right away. First, they need to find out everybody involved in the platform: the outfit that built it, the guys who serviced it, whoever made the safety and blowout equipment, that kind of thing. It'll probably all be in the papers, but they'd better search the internet too. Second, they need to get the clients onto the usual kind of fee contract. They can call Francel for that."

"Yes, boss." Tom sounded upbeat.

"And I guess you'd better come in here. We need to put our heads together. For one thing, I want to go see that platform before it gets demolished. With a good, knowledgeable guide. We'll need a helicopter, I guess. Not one of those little ones. A big one."

Tom got the idea. "A huge Sikorsky, or something else that won't make our sensitive stomachs airsick."

5

In Jimmy Coleman's huge corner office, the gold hardware glittered on his priceless Italian inlaid chest. Vines and flowers in red, brown, and green spread themselves across its honey-colored frame, set in the intarsiato style of Quattrocento artists. Nearby, the man himself sat behind a desk made in Tuscany with the same flowering vines.

"You know, Jennifer," Jimmy said to the associate sitting across from him in a desk chair with matching red, brown, and green vines, "this Deepwater Rose Case is going to be hard. We're going to have a dogfight trying to defend our good client, the Emerald Petroleum Company, after this offshore blowout."

Jennifer Lowenstein knew what that meant. Saying that the Emerald Petroleum Company was our "good client" didn't mean that it was well run, or financially sound, or a responsible corporate citizen. It meant that Emerald Petroleum paid millions a year to the law firm called Booker and Bayne without ever questioning the bill.

"Maybe so, Jimmy, but it's always a dogfight," she replied. "Why would this one be any different?"

"Because this one will be a reverse gangbang."

"What?"

"Something went wrong out there in Gulf-of-Mexico-Land. Somebody is likely to be found at fault."

"So why's that different from our usual case?"

"There will be a lot of defendants. And they will fight the plaintiffs. But at the same time, they will be falling all over themselves to point fingers at each other. The reverse of a gangbang. We will have to blame the plaintiffs, and blame the other defendants, and protect ourselves from all of them."

"Oh. I see."

"And our good client will not be easy to defend. The Emerald Petroleum Company has some expo-o-o-osure. Some real *expo-o-o-osure,* for sure."

Jennifer knew what this meant too, of course. Saying that the client had "some expo-o-o-osure" meant that it was guilty as sin. But Booker and Bayne would wrestle, twist, and spin to get it out of trouble. If the situation were not so bad, Jimmy would have used milder terms, like "a little bitty bit of expo-o-o-osure," or maybe even "some kinda minor wrinkle."

"What're we gonna do, then, Jimmy?"

"Try the victims. The plaintiffs, that is. And try all the bad guys. Meaning, try all the other defendants, because they automatically are the bad guys, to us. Try everybody in the case outside of our guys."

Jennifer laughed. For a former street fighter, Jimmy Coleman was a marvelous teacher. And everyone in the firm wanted to work for him, because all of your time got paid, even if you were a deadhead spectator at some obscure event.

At the same time, nobody knew how that primitive child named Jimmy, who had been, of all things, a gang member in south Los Angeles, had made it here. How he had been able to escape gang territory and graduate from college, much less the law school at UCLA, and become the present Jimmy Coleman, head of litigation at the big international law firm called Booker and Bayne.

"I'm following you, Jimmy." Jennifer was still laughing. "It's not hard to understand, even if it's going to be hard to do. Simple, in fact, at least in concept. A reverse gangbang. We just try everybody else."

* * *

The Sikorsky S-92 wavered a little in a clear air downdraft. "There it is," said Johnny Tull. "See that speck over there at one o'clock? That's the Emerald Rose."

"Not ... really. No, not yet, Johnny," Robert Herrick answered. "You're the expert, and you know where it is. I'm glad we have you along to tell us about the essential things that we don't know are essential because we can't see them."

The dusty dot on the horizon grew to an unmistakable structure in the sea during the next minute of travel, and then its shape and features gradually became visible.

"Notice that it's listing to north-northeast." Johnny pointed. "The moorings for the two legs on that side gave way during the explosion and fire. Ugly."

"It looks awful," Robert agreed. "You can see the crew quarters over there, opposite from the cranes."

"All black from the fire. Blacker than black."

"Blacker than a hundred midnights, down in a cypress swamp," Robert quoted.

That phrase was the best line ever written by the poet James Weldon Johnson, and it just popped out. Immediately, Robert thought: Here I am embarrassing myself by spouting poetry with a blue-collar crew on the way to an oil well. He laughed.

Johnny Tull stared at him, smiled, and said, "Ahhh . . . yes."

Robert just laughed at himself some more. "Since we can't land on the platform, let's descend to a few hundred feet and get close. And Johnny, please tell us what we're seeing."

"All right. The Emerald Rose, also known as the Deepwater Rose, was constructed in 2007 by Hyundai Heavy Industries in Korea. It's a deepwater rig set up as a compliant tower. A 'compliant tower' just means that it has legs anchored to the sea bed, but the legs are flexible, and the platform sways with prevailing currents. In other words, it's 'compliant' with the water. And it's designed to be used wherever you need it in the world: Malaysia, Brazil, or Norway. Or here."

Johnny pointed at the four columns below the platform that disappeared in the water. Then, he went on.

"The Emerald Rose is sited near the junction of the Keathley Underwater Canyon and the Alaminos Canyon, two hundred or so miles out into the Gulf of Mexico from Houston. The Alaminos Canyon also is the site of the Perdido Fold Belt, where some of the deepest wells in the Gulf are spotted. But the Emerald Rose is on the canyon slope and actually at the passage between the Keathley and the Alaminos, and so the water isn't nearly as deep."

"Tell us about the personnel," Tom Kennedy said.

"There were 127 workers of various occupations on the Emerald Rose when the explosion occurred. These included cooks, stewards, firefighters, and everybody else you need for an extended stay, in addition to the roughnecks who handled the drill stem. Most of them worked typical offshore shifts of two weeks off and two weeks on, so the entire force was much bigger, of course."

Now, the Sikorsky was still, just above the platform. The habitation, or living quarters, was the biggest structure on it, and the next largest was the operations center. The derrick was as far away from the habitation as it could be, but it was apparent that even with the size of this structure, human beings would be crowded here.

"The habitation's blast resistant, of course," Johnny Tull told them. "Notice that I say blast-resistant, not blast-proof. It is a miracle that the habitation didn't lose integrity. Then we coulda had more than a hundred dead, not just twenty-seven. They say that the explosion was visible more than forty miles away, even below the horizon."

"What companies were there?"

"The biggest group of people was from the Emerald Petroleum Company. But there were a substantial percentage from Dalliman Services, Momex Offshore, and Amadanko."

"The prospective defendants we knew about already. Good. So, Johnny, what happened? Why did the Emerald Rose blow up?"

"Nobody knows for sure yet."

"Oh, come on. Give us what you think probably happened."

"Well … This was a well that went down deep, and even if it wasn't the deepest in the water, the wellbore threaded way down farther, nearly two miles below the seabed. It's hard to work that depth. It's hard even to know what conditions are, except that you know it's going to be hot and have ungodly heavy pressure."

Johnny waved his arms. "Just after 9 o'clock at night on April 20, a plume of seawater blasted out of the marine riser. It shot almost 250 feet above the platform. Only one thing's going to do that: methane gas. And so next they got this pudding mixture of drilling mud, water, and gas. Methane in a liquid state, under tremendous pressure. The methane cleared its way, gasified, and caught a spark. There was a smaller explosion or two and then an all-enveloping fire."

He pointed at the habitation. "From there, they tried to activate the Annular Blowout Preventer. It failed. And then they tried the last resort, the Blind Shear Ram, and that didn't stop the well either.

"As for the twenty-seven who were killed—half of them, their bodies still haven't been recovered. Blown up and burned to bits and eaten by fishes. That included one of the several tool pushers on board. A 'tool pusher,' you know, is just oil field terminology for the head drilling guy. There were dozens of men injured too, and the rig was evacuated by sea."

Robert involuntarily bowed his head. "Twenty-seven dead. God rest their souls."

"So if you ask me, it's because of the Blowout Preventer and the Blind Shear Ram. Which didn't prevent. Or ram. So, you can ask Dalliman, Momex, and Amadanko.

"But then again, the reason was that the pressure outgunned all the safety stuff. And that's because of the whole enchilada, which was underequipped for the pressure. And mishandled, especially the drilling mud. And that—well, all of it was overseen by the Emerald Petroleum Company. That's who I'd say was the most guilty."

6

I love this baby," Robert Herrick said, as he steered his burgundy-colored Duesenberg northward on Kirby Drive. "This car just looks so great. And it sounds so great."

The bulging, curved hood of the car seemed to go on forever. Beneath it, twelve cylinders plunged and rose in perfect harmony. It cost a fortune to keep this Duesenberg running right, but when it was, the purr of the twelve sounded so much better than six. They blended in a throaty music that was louder and yet had more bass tones than any of his other cars, from the Testarossa to the '38 Packard.

"I've lost count of how many of these expensive dinosaurs you have." Maria Melendes sat in the front seat with her red hair flying. She laughed at him.

"I'm . . . not sure myself, except that I need to add onto the garage again. That building is actually the thing that's most expensive, much more than any of the cars. It's got more humidity and temperature controls than you'd have in a wine cellar. These cars are more than a hobby, or at least they're a hobby that costs me a lot."

His 1931 Stutz had a fold-down windshield and a true rumble seat. His 1930 Cadillac had an unbelievable sixteen cylinders that strummed like Niagara Falls but got eight miles to the gallon. The 1930 Bentley was once the favorite of James Bond, Agent 007, and Robert had one that was dark green.

"I know." She was still laughing. "You usually aren't ostentatious. In fact, you're sometimes slow to spend anything on small luxuries because you don't want to act like some of the rich and powerful people you dislike. But I guess these beautiful old cars are a whole other thing."

"As I've said before, after my two kids, these buggies are my biggest indulgence."

"Well," she answered, "I'm glad we're indulging the small luxury of taking in an opera tonight."

"It's about the fourth time they've done Aida in the last few years. Now, that is a girl who made a lot of bad choices. Aida, that is."

"Sure. A story has to have bad choices in it. Conflict. Adventure. Danger."

"And in Aida, death."

"That's right. You getting in the mood for this opera?"

"Yes. I'm well reminded of bad choices. For one thing, I understand that the head lawyer for the Emerald Petroleum Company is that fine citizen, Jimmy Coleman."

Her nose wrinkled, and she made a noise between a growl and a roar. "I didn't know that, when I encouraged you to take on this case. I thought it would involve more or less normal lawyers and give you a fun adventure."

"Bad choice?"

"Maybe."

* * *

Many miles to the southeast, the platform tender floated up toward the Emerald Rose Platform, and the engines shifted to hold it stationary. On board the ship there were three petroleum engineers, four crew, and ten black-suited lawyers. And Jimmy Coleman, who stood out in his seersucker suit.

"The drill stem is still attached to the platform," Jimmy said.

"See how the piping is bent?" said Axel Ibrahim, who was Jimmy's main expert here. "It looks perpendicular and goes down into the greenish seawater, there. But what you don't see is that it has a long, gradual curve all the way down to the sea floor."

"Dr. Ibrahim, I'd like you to tell us about the worst case against the Emerald Petroleum Company. The worst. We'll figure out the snappy comebacks to the worst case after that. But for now, tell us the story that makes Emerald look bad. The awful yarn that you'd spin if you were trying to pin it all on Emerald Petroleum."

"Well, I don't know about that. Dalliman Services is going to have a lot of responsibility because of the Blowout Preventer."

"Yes. We'll get to that later. But for now, talk to us about how the plaintiffs are going to load all the fault on Emerald Petroleum, because we know they'll be trying to do just that."

"Sure. To start with, this wasn't the first time. The Coast Guard had already investigated sixteen different fires and spills on board the Emerald Rose in the preceding seven years, when the platform traveled all around the world. That's a lot, but frankly, it sometimes happens with a platform like this, and none of those incidents has been connected by evidence to the big disaster. There was one major accident in its history, though. There was a time when it went through a drill stem occlusion, and a hundred or so people had to be evacuated."

The expert pointed at the leaning drill stem. "I bet you'll find something in the internal documents that says the Emerald Petroleum people debated about the casing. The lining of the wellbore. There'll probably be documents where engineers warned against it. That stuff was vulnerable to high pressure. You know that the operation was delayed, in fact way behind—more than a month—because of difficulties in transporting the rig here. That's not just a delay. It's a financial disaster. Millions a day, for this kind of rig."

"And so we're going to hear from the plaintiffs about hurry-up strategies that compromised safety."

"You can bet on it. And you already know about how the Blowout Preventer was leaking, and the VP of Production said go ahead anyway. Actually, it was a stack of Preventers, but we just call the whole stack a Blowout Preventer. And also, you know about how drilling mud was falling into the gas formation, which is a potential explosion because it can stop up the whole well and then release pressure all at once."

"And there was a pipe that fell in? Is that right?"

"That's right. A pipe fell into the well. That's not good. It can help to occlude the wellbore. In fact, the rig was experiencing what we call gas 'kicks' for several days before the blowout, meaning sharp gas releases."

"I guess the worst thing was that survey of the employees."

"Pretty troublesome. Yeah. An internal survey found out that the culture was stupidly anti-safety. Everybody was reacting to the time delay. The employees reported that they were afraid of retaliation if they said anything about glitches of any kind."

"There must have been warnings on the day of the explosion."

"Emerald Petroleum employees say they weren't aware of any-thing abnormal until the rig erupted. But hell's bells, they should have been. There was gas bubbling into the drill stem, and it showed on the readings, and that's a warning of a coming blowout. The VP of Produc-tion told the crew to replace some of the drilling mud with seawater to speed things up, even though the tool pusher yelled that it was a mistake. That guy took a risk with his protest, because everyone knew you could get fired for slowing things down with safety problems."

The expert gestured with his hand as if pushing something down. "And after all, it was that dense drilling mud that contained the gas pressure. You take that away—and boom."

"All right." Jimmy wasn't fazed by the bad news. "We'll find ways to say that all of this is speculation and just plain wrong."

He faced the engineer. "Now, Dr. Ibrahim, please tell us how to blame it all on Dalliman Services."

"Not much difficulty to that. Dalliman employees were the second most plentiful personnel, after the Emerald Petroleum people. And they were responsible for the Blowout Preventer. Now, here's how to make that argument against Dalliman. . . ."

* * *

The sun went down and the shadows deepened. Robert drove along Bellaire Boulevard and pulled into the parking lot. The sign said, "Sunrise Green Assisted Living. This Is Your Home." The sign was green, of course. And it featured a golden sunrise.

Robert walked along the corridor, all too aware of the antiseptic smell. It actually was more than antiseptic. It was a sensation, to Robert, that mixed medicinal unpleasantness with the smell of death. He had only been here a few times, but he knew he would be back often, and he hated the smell already.

The name plate said, "Rosalie Herrick." He knocked on the door.

"Come in."

"Hi, Mama," he said, in his most cheerful voice.

"Frederick! You look wonderful."

He hesitated. Then: "No, Mama." His voice was gentle, and he put a smile in it. "No. Frederick was my father. And your husband. I miss him. He is no longer with us."

"Oh."

"I'm Robert. I'm your son."

"I'm sorry. I'm so embarrassed. I get . . . all balled up, sometimes. They say it's hardening of the arteries. If I wait . . . . Well. . . . . Let's see if this feeling will go away. Good things come to she who waits."

"They" had told Robert, instead, that it was Alzheimer's disease, and it wouldn't go away. It would only get worse. But his mother was forever optimistic. Forever cheerful.

His father, Robert remembered, was the one who taught him things. His father was also the disciplinarian. His mother was the one who filled him with love.

"Mama, you've been here for two weeks now. Do you like it? Is it all right?"

He realized that his voice shook. He was anxious. Way too anxious.

But she laughed. "I told you I loved it, Robert, before I ever saw it! I already knew that I loved my room. I knew before I saw it. And I do love it, my little one. My little Robert."

He waited. He knew exactly what she would say next.

"I remember when you first described it to me, Robert. And I told you, the things in the room didn't matter." She laughed again. "It didn't matter about the embroidered curtains. Or the clear tan walls, or the tiles and carpet. Or the dining room with white tablecloths."

She smiled at him. "You can decide beforehand that you love it, or you can decide beforehand that you don't, and deciding that you don't is the same thing as deciding to be unhappy. I've always known that. And I decided beforehand that I loved my room. Before I even saw it."

He wondered whether she really knew who he was. But she went on. "I know that I have to be here. Because sometimes . . . I just get all balled up. But I love it here. I have friends, and they remind me of their names, just like you did." She laughed again, laughing at herself.

Now, she seemed excited, almost girlish. "What kind of work do you do, my Robert? Do you work?"

"Mama, I'm a lawyer."

"Oh, my. That sounds really fancy. But I'm sure it's fun. Is it fun, to you?"

He didn't know what to say. The truth was, it wasn't much fun these days. But he smiled. "Yes, Mama."

"Robert, your eyes are so blue."

"That's what I use to see with." Both of them laughed, because both of them liked being silly.

And he stayed there for a time, the way he'd done before and would do again in the future. It wasn't just a duty. It was really pretty pleasant. She talked and talked, and she was interesting. She was surprising. Sometimes she had memories that astounded him. And she asked him questions that he didn't know how to answer.

An hour and a half later, he left to drive home. For the thousandth time, he regretted not having his mother living with him, still. And he thought, "What I do as a lawyer . . . it ought to be fun."

And he thought, "I'm just going to flat-out *decide* that practicing law is fun. So that it'll come true."

But he doubted that he had the mental power that his mother could command.

7

So, we have a long list of plaintiffs, Tom, and we have to file our lawsuit. Here's our next question. Where do we file it?"

Robert sat at his desk, opposite Tom Kennedy. Chalky white clouds floated in a China blue sky, and the sun glinted off the downtown buildings. You could see forever through the floor-to-ceiling windows, out past the green of Memorial Park and all the way to a hazy gray horizon.

Tom shrugged. "I guess we can't file it where it happened, because that's in the middle of the Gulf of Mexico."

"Ahh, no. But it's going to be weird. Here's why."

Robert gestured with his hands outstretched. "The Emerald Rose is way out in the Gulf. Past the inner continental shelf. The states have jurisdiction over land under the ocean only up to three miles out. The Emerald Rose was way farther out in the ocean than that."

"So it's federal territory." Tom nodded. "The lands under the Emerald Rose, the sea bed canyons, are owned by the United States. Just like Yosemite National Park."

"That's right."

"And we'll end up in federal court. Where no plaintiff ever wants to be. Federal court."

"That's right too. In federal court, you get procedured to death. And delayed to death. But yes, unfortunately, we'll end up in federal court. Even if we file our lawsuit in state court, like we'd like to do, the defendants would be sure to remove the case to federal court so they could use all that nifty federal confusion to run us around the maypole."

"And I guess we have federal law there, too, since the explosion was on federal land." Tom shook his head. "The feds are always against us."

"Well, that's interesting. We do have federal law out there deep in the ocean, but here's what's weird. The federal law that covers the Emerald Rose is actually . . . state law."

Tom stared. "Come again?"

"Federal law isn't a complete body of law. For instance, there's not general federal law that covers a car wreck or a simple contract. So the federal law adopts the law of the state. The law of what's called the 'upland state'—the state that would have jurisdiction if there were state jurisdiction out in the ocean that far. That state law becomes the federal law."

"I wish I followed you."

"The law is federal law. That's what the law is, that covers a platform on the outer continental shelf. Like the Emerald Rose."

"Right. Got that."

"But the federal government has never adopted any law to cover accidents. There's no federal law out in the Gulf of Mexico like what we call negligence law. All the federal government does is to say that the federal law on a platform out there is the law of the upland state. So, it's our state law, good old Texas law, which automatically becomes federal law, and that's what covers this blowout and explosion."

Tom shook his head. "Let me see if I've got it. It's state law that covers the Emerald Rose, but that's because the state law becomes federal law, and federal law is the kind of law that covers this oil well platform?"

"You've got it, Tom."

"Again, because I'm still trying to absorb it. The law is federal law, but the federal law just happens to be state law because there isn't any other federal law, and the federal government adopts state law to cover the gap."

"Correct. The technical term is that the law covering the Emerald Rose is *borrowed* state law. The state law applies because magically, the feds borrow state law, and it becomes federal law."

"Sheesh."

"Well, it's not that much of a problem. What it means is that we tell the jury about the law in the same way we'd tell them in state court."

"And first step is, we file it in federal court. Step two is, state law applies. Step three is that state law becomes federal law. And step four is, since we're in federal court, our case, which is governed by state law, will be handled by federal procedure, under the Federal Rules of Civil Procedure. "

"Right. With lots of potential for rules that don't fit."

"Yes."

"So, Tom, it's not ideal, but start making the suit papers. I mean, the Complaint. And we'll file them right here in town, at the federal courthouse."

Tom laughed. "Are you sure you wanted to be talked into taking this case, Robert? Because I bet this is just the start of a whole bunch of upside-down stuff."

"Right again. This case is going to look like Alice in Wonderland. And then it probably will take us, together with Alice, all the way Through the Looking Glass."

* * *

Out on the Continental Shelf, the tilted plane of the Emerald Rose was quiet. Quick, heroic efforts had stopped the oil flow. The spill had been captured or dispersed. And now, for some reason, the location was a favorite of fishing vessels. It wasn't just because fish tended to congregate around abandoned structures. This one had four slender pilings and a drill stem extending into the water. There were fish, yes, but not as many as crowded around more dense structures near the surface, in shallower water.

Maybe people sailed here because the platform marked a place where the ocean depth changed. Places like that were thought to be good fishing sites, whether that was right or wrong. Or maybe it was because it was a gathering place, a place that you could assume there would be others doing the same thing. A social place. And maybe it was just plain curiosity.

Fishing boats pulled in snapper, puffer, trout, and croaker here. There were occasional grouper too. The northwestern side of the rig, where the platform leaned most toward the water, was better because the ocean there was shallower. The Emerald Rose, after all, did not stand on a canyon floor. It was up high on the canyon ridge.

But fishing wasn't the only activity here.

There also was the illegal drug trade. This was a less publicized use of the doomed and blackened platform. Cocaine and heroin changed hands here, especially during the dark of the night, after midnight, or sometimes at first light. The custom was for a Mexican vessel from Tamaulipas State, where the drug business flourished and life was cheap, to visit the platform when it was clear of other traffic.

That vessel, from Mexico, would transfer the precious cargo to a vessel from the United States—a ship with Texas, Mississippi, or Louisiana registration. Each time, a different vessel came from each side, and the exchange took place at a different hour each time. The more careful way to do it was for the Mexican smugglers to attach the load to the leaning platform of the Emerald Rose and for the North American sailors to pick it up there.

The slanted rig was hard to access, and it was blackened and crumbling in places, but the method worked, and it was less likely than overland travel to be intercepted by law enforcement. The Mexican vessel returned to its port, and the United States vessel to its port, with nothing to call attention to either voyage.

The Tamaulipas capos, or *jefes*, were proud of their trade secret. After all, the cartels had used much more expensive and dangerous methods from time to time. The cartels had been known to use jerry-rigged submarines, not to mention tunnels multiple miles long. The Emerald Rose exchange furnished a low-budget conveyance, and it was much more practical and much less subject to loss than a lot of other delivery systems.

It worked fine, that is, until Robert Herrick took his second helicopter trip to visit the Emerald Rose.

* * *

Two hundred miles away from the burned platform, Jennifer Lowenstein sat in Jimmy Coleman's office, in one of the desk chairs with red, brown, and green vines that matched the pattern on Jimmy's priceless Italian chest. She looked puzzled, like a non-mathematician trying to follow a chain of calculus equations, or maybe a non-accountant trying to understand how inventory is valued.

"So, it doesn't matter whether we're in federal court or state court, the law is the same, and it's federal law, but the federal law is state law."

"Right." Jimmy's voice grated pleasantly, because a lawyer always enjoys being the only one in the room who understands a complicated problem.

"The plaintiffs can file this case in state court, but we can remove it to federal court. But even then, we still get state law in federal court, because state law becomes federalized."

"Right again." Jimmy showed his dirty teeth. "The law stays the same, but it matters to us which court we're in. The federal court is what we want. The federal court will use the Federal Rules of Civil Procedure to handle the case, even though it applies state law. Being in federal court will give us all kinds of opportunities for confusion and delay."

"So, if it's filed in state court, we're going to join together all the defendants and remove it to federal court."

"Right. You know, I read this little essay by Professor Michael Maslanka, who explained it all pretty well. The Professor says you are always better in a federal court if you are the defendant. Going to the federal building, he says, is 'not unlike entering a cathedral.' There will be all kinds of hocus-pocus available to us. We can play all kinds of tricks on the plaintiffs."

Jennifer smiled.

"So, let's plan ahead. The plaintiffs will file suit either in federal court or state court. They might figure out that we'd remove it to federal court if they filed in state court, and so they might file it in federal court just to avoid some of the delay and confusion that's caused by that kind of removal. If they do that, we just defend the suit there in federal court. With all the tricks and traps. But the plaintiffs will prefer state court. In case they file it there, Jennifer, get ready to remove it to federal court."

"Where we can twist and turn the issues." Jennifer laughed. "And we can get an army of associates to think up new ways to make the case even more complicated."

"Right."

"I'm on it, Jimmy."

* * *

Robert Herrick turned and looked out the big windows bordering his office. Way down below, the ant-like cars crawled on tiny freeways. The sun was setting heavily on the shoulder of Memorial Park, turning the sky from blue to pink, red, and yellow.

"So, Tom, we'd better just file our lawsuit in federal court against all the Emerald Rose defendants. If we filed it in state court, the defendants would remove it to federal court right away."

"And there would be a twilight zone, while the lawsuit would be in two different courts at the same time. Which would allow the defendants to stir up even more delay and confusion than they'd create if we were in federal court in the first place."

"Right. So, Tom, you might as well get to work putting together the Complaint that we're going to file in our friendly local federal court."

"Okay. Will do."

"And by the way, Tom, we ought to go out to the Emerald Rose another time. Not immediately, but soon. Let's arrange the big helicopter again. I learned a lot from the first trip, but I've got a bunch of new questions."

"I'm on it, Robert."

8

The law clerk had graduated at the top of his class at Harvard Law School. That did not mean, however, that he'd gotten a good education. As is customary in elite law schools, he had taken a course in Contracts without ever seeing a contract, a course in Wills without ever seeing a will, and a course in Torts without ever seeing a negligence complaint. After graduation, these prestigiously educated lawyers fanned out all over the country, from Maine to California, and became legal advisers to federal judges. A sought-after first job.

Now, as he walked into the judge's spacious chambers, the law clerk carried a sheaf of papers. "Judge, the luck of the draw says that you are presiding over the Emerald Rose case. You know, that explosion on the oil platform."

United States District Judge Pamela Preston looked up sharply. "Oh, no. I think I might want to retire instead."

"Really? It sounds interesting." The law clerk was new, and he didn't yet know that judges usually do not favor the most contentious and complicated cases.

"Not really. No." The judge laughed. "But I was hoping for a few little cases involving simple jury trials in the near future. That big patent case we just finished—it ate me up. Patent attorneys are the most combative lawyers in the whole profession, and I had to learn all about the software industry to understand that case. And now I get the Emerald Rose case. And I guess I'll have to learn all about the technicalities of offshore production."

"Well, but the case isn't raising issues about offshore production, not yet." The law clerk stared at the papers. "First, there's this strange kind of Motion. The defendant's answers aren't even due yet, but they've filed something called a Motion to Preserve Evidence. I've never heard of such a thing."

Judge Preston started to say something disparaging about how little anybody hears about anything important at Harvard Law School, where they study a particular professor's concepts of "fairness" instead of studying Contracts, and they discuss "the right to counsel" instead of Litigation Procedure. But she opted, instead, for a kinder approach. These law clerks were supposed to be helping her, even though it sometimes felt as though she were teaching law school courses to them.

"Well, I haven't heard of that kind of Motion very often either," the judge said in a soothing voice. "A Motion to Preserve Evidence, that is. It comes up sometimes, but not very often. Who are the lawyers?"

"The Plaintiffs' Complaint was filed by someone named Robert Herrick."

"That's okay. He'll be competent, and he won't lie to the court."

"And this Motion to Preserve Evidence was filed by a lawyer named . . . ." The law clerk looked at the end of the document. ". . . Jimmy Coleman, out of Booker and Bayne."

"Uggggh." The judge's smile faded.

* * *

"Robert, you won't believe what's happening in the Emerald Rose case." Tom Kennedy walked across the colorful oriental carpet toward his senior partner. "I mean, the weird stuff is already appearing."

"What's that?"

It was raining buckets and barrels outside. Water slapped against the greenhouse windows. The shadows on the oriental carpet were muted, even where it slipped out from the pink and red geraniums.

"First thing," Tom frowned, "guess who represents Emerald Petroleum. It's your old friend, Jimmy Coleman, from good old Booker and Bayne."

"Uggggh." This time, it was Robert's smile that faded.

"He hasn't filed an answer to the lawsuit yet. The answer's not due until next week. But he's filed this nutty kinda Motion."

"What sort of nutty kinda Motion?"

"It's called a Motion to Preserve Evidence. And it goes on for page after page."

"What's it want us to preserve, allegedly?"

"Well, it starts with medical records. What Jimmy says is allegedly true, which is that these are needed for defense against personal injury or death claims. I imagine so. But I've never seen a motion directed to the individual plaintiffs to preserve those kinds of records. You get complete records only from the doctors and hospitals."

"Neither have I. But I can guess why Jimmy's doing it. By now, we have literally hundreds of individual clients in this case. Just communicating with them, not to mention getting them to search and retain everything, would be a backbreaking job. Jimmy wants us to spin our wheels for a lot of wasted time, and he thinks that way we'll get distracted from the important things."

"Well, yes, and medical records are just the beginning of the list of stuff. The Motion asks us to get each individual plaintiff to preserve every paper relating to any kind of exercise done. And any kind of athletic or sports activity. And any travel. And any blah, blah, and blah, for five single-spaced pages, on and on."

"Okay. Tom, we're going to oppose this Motion. Here's what you need to do. First, figure out a quick and dirty estimate of how much time it would take the average adult to compile all of the papers or electronics he or she might have, all of them, all of the types that are described within this Motion. Then, figure out what we would have to do to get all of our hundred-plus clients to do it, and how much attorney time it would take us."

"I'm on it."

"I'm not quite through. Also, figure out what alternative places the defendants could get all this stuff from. And finally, take a guess at how much admissible and useful evidence this Motion really would be likely to produce."

"Okay. Tom laughed.

* * *

"Robert Herrick has filed an Opposition to the Motion to Preserve Evidence." Judge Pamela Preston's law clerk sounded . . . uncertain. Because he was . . . uncertain. "And Jimmy Coleman has filed a Response to the Opposition."

"Okay." The judge scanned the clerk's memorandum with a practiced eye. "First of all, you're right about the limits of what Coleman can get. The Rule says that document production has to be 'proportional' to the needs of the case. *Proportional.* And this is a pretty long list for something that has to be proportional."

"Well, the defendants—Mr. Coleman, that is—say that this is just a Motion to Preserve Evidence, not actual document production. He says, because it's not actual document production but only preserving stuff, the proportionality standard doesn't apply. And he says, anyway, it's a huge case and it's naturally going to involve a lot of documents."

"So, he's saying that since he's not asking for the documents to be handed over, even though they wouldn't do him any good unless they were handed over, he should be able to get the plaintiffs to spend a *disproportionate* amount of time and money? Which would defeat the purpose of the Rule?"

"I guess so." The law clerk was still confused about the right answer. "And the plaintiffs estimate that the typical individual plaintiff would have to spend more than twenty hours to find all of this stuff. Multiplied over a hundred individuals, that's two thousand man-hours. And they estimate that to get a hundred non-lawyers to comply with a requirement like this, and to assure that they've all done it, would take at least a hundred hours of attorney time. Which, at market rates, would cost at least $250,000."

"That's the way to measure proportionality." The judge nodded. "And that's the way to inform the judge."

"So, judge, do you think you will deny the Motion to Preserve, then?"

"Mostly, yes. This is just plain overreaching by Jimmy Coleman." Judge Preston thought for a moment. "This will be an unusual order. But here's what I want to do. Write up an order that denies the Motion, with one exception. Medical and health care records during the last five years. The plaintiffs are ordered to preserve any medical and health care records, in any form including electronic records if there are any—but only records that they individually possess, and that can be retrieved with a search not exceeding one hour per individual."

"Yes, your honor."

"And write it so that the denial of everything else makes it clear that the judge does not approve of this tactic, without saying so directly. I want to head off any more Jimmy Coleman sleaze before it happens. As they said in the Wild West, I want to head off this kind of stuff at the pass."

"Yes, your honor."

"And now, we'll follow the ancient political credo. We'll leave all of this behind us and handle everything in the future as though this dumb-ass Motion hadn't been filed. But we keep a memory of what happened, in case there's more sleaze. In fact, there's a little proverb about this, about what to do in this situation. About what to do about folks like Jimmy Coleman when they get caught pulling little dirty tricks that you can't really punish them for."

"What's that proverb, judge?" The law clerk thought he was going to hear something like an important rule of law. "What's the proverb?"

"Forgive." The judge smiled, and nodded. "We need to forgive . . . and *REMEMBER*."

9

The big helicopter descended to two thousand feet as they approached the Emerald Rose. Robert and Tom stared at the platform. It was barely dawn, the best time to hire this Sikorsky.

"Now that we know a little more, we can talk a little more intelligently about what happened to the Blowout Preventer," said Johnny Tull, their offshore expert.

"Well, but look. There's something weird going on." Robert pointed. "There's this guy on the platform. Standing on the platform. Standing on it, while it's leaning all out of kilter. What's he doing?"

Tom gestured at a boat that stood nearby from Tamaulipas, Mexico. "That must be how he got here."

"The guy on the platform is attaching some kind of . . . something . . . to one of the cranes. Is that what he's doing?"

"Yes, but it's hard to tell what it is he's tying down onto the crane."

The pilot had been a Coast Guard airman in an earlier career. "Can't be sure, but I can tell you this. It's not any part of any government investigation, and that guy is not from any of the drilling outfits, either."

"What is it, then?"

"I'll bet you a hundred bucks and a whiskey that it's drug trade. If folks from the states were putting it on the platform, I'd bet that it'd be assault rifles. But with a ship from Mexico, it's going to be heroin. Or cocaine. Not marijuana, because that would be much bigger than this—more bulky."

"Makes . . . sense, I guess."

The pilot was on the radio. "Come in, Coast Guard. This is Port Arthur Aviation C-6669. Suspect drug smuggling activity, Emerald Rose platform. Repeat, suspect drug smuggling activity, Emerald Rose platform."

A moment later, the radio crackled. "Port Arthur C-6669, this is Coast Guard Cutter Bernard C. Webber, WPC 1101. What's your 20?"

"Emerald Rose platform. Repeat, Emerald Rose platform." Quickly, the pilot described the scene.

"Ten-four, Port Arthur Aviation. Cutter Bernard C. Webber, en route."

"That's a Sentinel-class Fast-Response Cutter, that Bernard C. Webber," said the pilot. "A ship built for just this kind of chase."

"Look." Robert pointed. Here's another ship approaching. But this one looks like a vessel from the States, instead."

The pilot radioed this information to the Cutter.

Suddenly, there was a loud, fast series of cracking noises. "They're shooting at us!" someone said. The pilot turned the Sikorsky and streaked away. "An hour or so we'll be back on dry land."

"I guess we'll discuss the Blowout Preventer another time," said Johnny Tull. Wisely.

*   *   *

"The judge ruled against us." Jennifer Lowenstein sounded disappointed. "On the Motion to Preserve Evidence."

"Not exactly." Jimmy Coleman's voice was as coarse as usual, but he smiled. "The judge gave us part of what we wanted. And it's almost as good as what we wanted."

"She gave us only the tiniest part."

"But it's enough. That order is going to distract Herrick's team, real bad. As I say, we got most of what we wanted. They'll have to contact more than a hundred people. Herrick will have almost as much trouble as if the whole thing had been granted. And those people are going to feel harassed. It's part of the wear-'em-down strategy."

"Oh."

Jimmy and Jennifer sat opposite each other on the honey-colored chairs that had inlaid red, brown, and green flowers. The day outside was brilliant, without a cloud. The southern view of the city, out the big windows in Jimmy's corner office, showed traffic stalled on the elevated freeway and sun echoing off the buildings.

"The judge probably felt she was ruling in favor of Herrick," Jimmy croaked. "But this was an unusual Motion we filed, especially with the kind of stuff we asked the plaintiffs to find. I wouldn't have been surprised to have the whole thing denied, because it was just something I wanted us to try. Now, I bet Herrick is unhappy, which is the point."

"Oh. But . . . Jimmy, look here. The order from the judge says all kinds of bad stuff about our Motion. And about us. Such as that this kind of aggressive pushing is 'not favored by the Court.'"

"Judges say that kind of thing all the time, but she's actually done as much for us as we had any right to expect. See, Jennifer, people think that judges rule on the law. The letter of the law, they think. But half of the decisions a judge makes are purely discretionary. The judge just decides, without any law or guidelines behind it, because what to do is up to the judge."

"Well . . . yes."

"And in that situation, guess what judges do? They tend to compromise. To split the baby. To give something to each side. They say, in effect, 'You get some, and since I've given you some, I'll give some to the other side.' And I bet that's what the judge did here. She denied most of it but gave us a little piece. And it's a win for us. Or rather, it splits the baby, which means the side that wanted to have the baby split wins. Which, fortunately for us, is us."

"But what about the judge's order, which looks like she's mad at us? Will she be against us in the future?"

"If you're a winner, you've gotta be aggressive, Jennifer. And you've got to get used to the judge giving you a tongue lashing. We're going to get thrashings from judges a lot harder than this, now and then. If you're a winner, you know that's what happens, and you ignore it."

Jimmy's smile grew bigger, and his voice scratched harder. "If you're a winner, you take your shot, even if the judge doesn't like it, and you let the judge's venom just roll off your back."

* * *

Across town, sitting across from Tom Kennedy, Robert Herrick frowned. "Complying with this order from the judge is going to be a royal pain. I mean, preserving all this stuff, all the plaintiffs' health care records that they have."

"I know. We're going to have to assign a couple of lawyers and legal assistants immediately."

Outside Robert's office, the sun was in the west, filling the floor-to-ceiling windows. The greensward of Buffalo Bayou shone, and the view went all the way to the horizon. The traffic was stopped on the freeways, so many floors below.

"And the wording of this order makes it seem that the judge thought she was ruling in our favor."

"She wasn't, for sure. We'll have to set up a telephone room, as we've done before when we've had to communicate with a big group of individuals."

"And keep all kinds of records so that we can prove we complied. I guess it's not surprising. The judge told a clerk to write this order without thinking about it, because judges make so many decisions that they have to do that. They have to shoot from the hip."

"Right."

Tom shook his head. "I bet the judge didn't add up how much effort this is going to take."

"All right. So, Tom, get it started. Get two lawyers and two paralegals. Write up a suggested speech for all of them to make to each individual plaintiff. Set it up so that three of them, two legal assistants and a lawyer, can make calls. There needs to be one lawyer available to take a call any time a legal assistant gets in too deep and finds that people's questions call for legal advice."

"Yessir."

"And we've got to treat this as just something we knew we'd have to go through. In fact, we did expect it from Jimmy Coleman, you and I both. It's important that our lawyers not get discouraged or feel abused by this order, no matter what you and I think about it. We'll get through this and get back to vigorously pursuing this case."

* * *

His wife's call came through while Robert was deep in thought about what to do next in the Emerald Rose case.

"Hi, Maria. . . . What's up, Baby?"

"It's about your daughter, and it's awful. Pepper called and told me she got arrested late last night."

A pause. " . . . Arrested? For what?"

"Intoxication assault. If you're driving while intoxicated and you injure someone in a wreck, you can be guilty of intoxication assault. Which is a bigger crime than plain old driving while intoxicated. Pepper can't tell us how bad the injuries are to the other driver, but the poor guy is in the hospital. And it's going to be very serious for her, too."

"Tell me, just how serious do you think it'll be?"

"Well, it's worse than it might otherwise be, not only because of the injuries, but also because Pepper's been convicted of driving while intoxicated before."

Another pause. "That's . . . news to me."

"She pled guilty in that earlier case and managed to get through all the court proceedings without her daddy ever finding out. Your daughter hid it from you."

"Ahhhhhrg. . . ."

"She's out now, on bond. The bail is a substantial cost. I mean, the bond premium is usually ten percent, whether you're guilty or not."

"I know. Pepper is . . . well, to put it directly, she's had a lot of trouble that she's made herself. She's the same daughter who stole our credit card a few years ago and shared it with all her friends. She's the one who got pregnant in the middle of high school. She's the one . . . ."

"I know. And it's tempting to say, 'She got herself into this mess, and maybe it would be a learning experience for her to get out of it by herself.'"

"Tempting, yes, But that's not what I'm thinking, of course. She couldn't get the kind of lawyer I'd want her to have if we gave up on her. And this is a life-ruining situation. I'm just lamenting the situation. Which is not very useful."

"Well, we can get a lawyer who can help her. A good lawyer."

"Where is she right now?"

"At home."

"I'm going to leave the office and go see her. I've got a lot to do, but nothing that has to be done today."

"Okay." Maria's voice sounded tired. "But go easy on her. She's already been through plenty of stuff that's going to teach her a lesson. She doesn't need a lot more pain right now."

Being a lawyer doesn't mean that you're exempt from legal problems, he thought to himself as he drove home. And being a lawyer doesn't make you immune to family troubles.

If anything, it makes them worse.

10

The mountains in western Tamaulipas had very few inhabitants, which was the way El Raton preferred them. His real name was Enrico Pedro Nunez Rodriguez y Cavazos, but he had picked up the nickname playing soccer as a kid because he was sneaky and fast. He still liked being called El Raton. *The Mouse.* Quiet, sneaky, dangerous.

But right now, El Raton didn't like anything. He stomped up and down the great room in his hacienda, waving his arms and generally going ballistic over what he was hearing.

"How the hell did this happen?" he wanted to know.

His retainers were loyal because they valued their lives, but they had come as a group of six and were shaking with fear.

And this was also because they valued their lives.

"*Jefe*, Boss . . . , there was a helicopter, we heard."

A second voice spoke next. These cautious drugistas hoped that if they divided the story up, maybe they could avoid responsibility. "We don't know, but maybe the helicopter was just some Gringos looking into the Emerald Rose explosion. The helicopter watched our crew unload the goods from our delivery vessel."

A pause, and then a third voice. "And these Gringos in the helicopter, they got this Coast Guard warship to come there, a Coast Guard cutter, before our partners from the *Estados Unidos* could pick up the goods."

El Raton's Tamaulipas mountain compound was enormous, with an indoor pool, a bowling alley, and an archery range. Nearby, there were quarters for an army of cartel soldiers and a small town's worth of support personnel. The great room was built of limestone, with cedar rafters and elegant chandeliers. The walls were adorned with photographs of El Raton meeting with former Mexican Presidents, actors, and bishops.

"Why didn't our ship from the States chase the Coast Guard away?" El Raton wanted to know.

Another pause, and a fourth unidentifiable voice. "Our people had assault rifles, which were modified to automatic, but these were just small arms. Our delivery is designed to avoid attracting attention, and we don't have fixed guns on our watercraft."

And a fifth voice. "The Coast Guard is so, so much more powerful. This Sentinel-class cutter has a remote-operated 25 mm autocannon. And four crew-served Browning M2 machine guns."

El Raton knew it all, of course, because he took pride in having thought up this ingenious method of drug smuggling, involving two ships and an abandoned platform on each cross-border trip.

"A hundred thousand dollars' worth of cocaine gone." He stomped some more. "Just disappeared. A hundred thousand! And the worst part is, we can't use the Emerald Rose platform anymore."

"Perhaps no, Jefe."

"Who was this? Who was in the helicopter?" El Raton was determined to zero in on the real criminal, the one who had made him lose his goods and ruined his outstanding business method.

"All we know is that this helicopter was a dark red color and had something on it about a city. A city of 'Port Arthur,' in the United States."

El Raton stomped, but he was thinking while he stomped. His underlings stood quietly, hoping that whatever summary justice might be coming would not land upon them.

Finally, El Raton spoke. "I want to know who did this. First of all, find out about this dark red Port Arthur helicopter. And then, I want to know who was directing that aircraft. *Estes personas son muertas.* They're dying."

He put his hand under his chin and paused. Then, he spoke evenly, reasonably, because he viewed himself as a careful man, and he had thought the problem through prudently. Reasonably. Thoroughly, in a businesslike manner, which told him that the solution was a familiar one.

Assassination.

"I'm a businessman." He waved his arms, to emphasize how clear it all was. "I have to protect my business. And in this business, you can't just put up with it if someone screws up your operation and makes you lose your products. You have to do something about it. Fast. You've got to get that worm who's insulted you out of the picture. Permanently. And you have to do it in a way that tells everybody you are a man of fidelity. A sensible man, who protects his business."

* * *

"Robert, we ended up with a lot of loose ends." The two lawyers who had had the unpleasant job of contacting every single plaintiff were in his office now.

"Of course. I expected that. Tell me about it."

"The judge's order says we're supposed to preserve anything related to 'medical care or health care.' But exactly what does that mean? Where's the line drawn, as to what is heath care and what's not?"

"I know, I know, there are ambiguities. That's one of the things Jimmy Coleman intended to do, to worry us. So, what, for example?"

"Well, there were a couple of our plaintiffs who keep daily diaries. The diaries tell how they felt on some days and tell about going to the doctor, or relatives going to the doctor. They wanted to know, do we need to separate these diaries out and stack them up with the other stuff?"

"No," said Robert, without hesitation.

"They don't want their diaries read."

"And they don't have to put up with that. What else?"

"Some of them wanted to know about drug bottles. These little bottles have labels on them, and the labels have information."

Robert sighed. "No. That's ridiculous. Again, Jimmy Coleman wants us to stop preparing our lawsuit and get into debating nonsense, just like this. What else?

"There are some folks we can't get hold of by phone. And . . . well, there were a couple of our clients who just flat refused to do this, to chase after a bunch of will o' the wisps like this."

"And again, these are the kinds of time-wasting searches Jimmy Coleman was hoping to rope us into. The non-responses, unlike the other stuff you mentioned, are a problem. First, try to contact the ones you couldn't get hold of, by another phone call, and if that doesn't work, by email and certified letter. Ask them to call you, giving your name. Second, contact the ones who refused. Send both an email and a certified letter. Tell them the judge has ordered it and enclose a copy of the order. But be diplomatic with all of them."

"You think that will work?"

"The judge's order requires us to report, but only about the directions we've given our clients. Yes, I think it will work. We don't have to tattle on the ones who said no or who didn't pick up the phone. That always happens, with any big group of clients."

He smiled. "You two have done a good job. And it's a thankless task, as they say. But you have my thanks, even if it's a thankless task."

The two lawyers laughed at that.

After they left, Robert sighed again. "Jimmy won this one," he said to himself. "We've mostly gotten it done, but he's already distracted us and gotten us to waste thousands of dollars."

* * *

Across town, Jimmy Coleman stepped through the big glass doors with gold lettering that said, "Booker and Bayne." He walked across the cushy beige-and-gold carpet into the office of the big law firm.

As far as the eye could see, the floor was covered by secretarial bays crafted in white birch. The wood had come from a single stand of trees in Vermont. Across from the bays, toward the windows, the lawyers' offices were lined up, also sporting white birch trim, with partners having big spaces, located according to seniority and client relationships—the big business-getters in the corners, and associates in smaller ones.

Walking down the hallway, Jimmy heard the sounds of Booker and Bayne lawyers at work. Making stupendous amounts of money per hour. For that matter, making stupendous amounts of money per minute.

Findlay James, who was an oil and gas lawyer, was yelling at somebody, some unfortunate recipient of a telephone call. "You bet your ass, that acreage is held by production! If you explore that, we'll sure appreciate it, because we'll own whatever you find."

Jimmy laughed. The people Findlay dealt with probably assumed his bark was worse than his bite, but that ancient saying didn't apply.

Findlay's agressiveness in follow-up litigation was legendary within the firm. In other words, his bite actually was worse.

A few doors down, Sarah Gastwite was talking to an associate. "With this stuff we got in discovery, we can file a Motion for Summary Judgment and kick their tails all the way to Timbuktu."

Maybe, Jimmy thought. But to be able to say maybe, in some cases, is good enough. If the other side survives it, they'll be so beaten up that they'll settle for anything.

"Hi, Lisa," he said finally, when he reached his office at the other corner of the hallway.

"Jimmy! We missed you." His six-foot secretary hugged him. Jimmy, at five feet nine, was known to favor tall women, but that wasn't the only reason Jimmy valued this one. Lisa could type fast, take dictation fast, tell which phone calls were important, get rid of the other calls, and keep her cool when Jimmy involved her in his next shady deal.

"You want Jennifer?" asked Jimmy's secretary. His beautiful Amazon.

"Yes, indeed. Please get her."

And this directive from Jimmy set in motion a call from Lisa that would have Jennifer Lowenstein climbing three floors of stairs as fast as she could rather than waiting for the elevator. Just as she always did when Jimmy called.

11

Minutes later, Jennifer sat opposite Jimmy, in front of the Italian chest with its red, brown and green flowers. She was out of breath.

"Here's an idea, Jennifer." Jimmy's voice scraped as usual, but pleasantly this time. "Have a couple of associates look into this. And they should study the statute and the cases. My idea is simple."

Jennifer sat forward. She looked like a soldier sitting at attention.

Jimmy showed his brown teeth. "We can claim that every worker on the platform was a so-called 'borrowed servant' of the Emerald Petroleum Company."

"Every worker was a . . . what?"

"A borrowed servant of the Emerald Petroleum Company. They all worked for Emerald on that platform, even if Emerald just borrowed them from Dalliman and the other companies. That's the reality of the situation, you know. Emerald ran the show and controlled every worker who was there. Down to the cooks. Or at least, that's our argument."

"What good will that do?"

Jimmy laughed. "Borrowed servant law doesn't come up much in what we usually do here at Booker and Bayne. But I'm talking about the law of worker's compensation. If an injury is covered by worker's compensation insurance, that's all the worker collects. All he gets is worker's compensation insurance. He can't sue and get damages."

"Well, but that's a big amount, for twenty-seven dead guys. And there's no defense to worker's compensation insurance, is there?"

"No. That's right. You get it if you're injured on the job, because it's insurance. It's not a claim like negligence that lets the defendant defend by saying that we weren't negligent, or that the plaintiff was contributorily negligent. Which would be a tough argument anyway, since the dead guys, all they did was stand there on the platform."

"But what good does that do us? What good does it do, to claim they were all covered by our worker's comp insurance?"

"If an injury is covered by worker's compensation, the worker can't sue the employer."

"Oh." The light was finally starting to dawn, for Jennifer. "Okay."

"And so if we controlled all of the employees, or more technically, if they were all 'borrowed servants' of ours, we owe them nothing but worker's comp insurance. Which is peanuts compared to the damages in a civil suit. As I recall from the last time I saw it, death benefits were in the range of fifty thousand bucks. As opposed to millions per person in a lawsuit, which is what Herrick's going to want."

"What about the other companies? Dalliman and Momex Off-shore? And Amadanko?"

"Well, if this worker's comp defense works for us, it will take away the worker's comp defense for all those other companies. But there's a silver lining for them. They can blame it on us—on Emerald—and reduce their damages accordingly. And we'll help them do that."

"How will we help them?"

"By what's going to happen normally anyway. By the fact that the jury's likely to put the biggest percentage of fault on us. On Emerald Petroleum. And that reduces the damages that Dalliman and Momex and Amadanko will owe. I expect these other companies to oppose us, but as I say, there's a silver lining in it for them, and so I think they'll temper their fight against us."

"Wow."

"So, let's have the associates work on it. I understand the broad outlines of this worker's comp defense, but I'm not sure of the details. Have the associates look into what makes a person a 'borrowed servant' of another employer who's not his own employer."

"Okay, Jimmy. Let me see whether I understand it right. We—Emerald—had employees on the platform. But a lot of the people there were employees of other companies, like Dalliman. Still, we're going to claim that those other workers were really *our* employees—employees of Emerald—because Emerald Petroleum controlled what they did. And that means that they were *borrowed servants* of Emerald."

She paused for an instant. Then: "And since we say everyone on the platform was a 'borrowed servant' of Emerald, nobody can sue us for damages. All they get it worker's compensation. Which is a small fraction of the damages that we would owe in a negligence lawsuit. Emerald owes a little, or actually, its insurers owe something, but we win big."

"Right. That's exactly it, Jennifer. But put some associates onto researching the details."

"You got it, Jimmy. I'm on my way."

* * *

Meanwhile, a mile to the north, the Criminal Justice Building was ringed by protesters carrying signs. There were men, women, and a few children, dressed in dirty blue jeans, shorts, and tank tops, all yelling. Assistant District Attorney Maria Melendes gingerly made her way through the moving, jumping, shouting bodies, up to the courthouse steps. She was wearing big sunglasses and a nondescript jacket.

She made out some of the words in the roar of the crowd. "Free Homer! Free Homer!" One of the signs said, "Justice for Homer Harding." Another one said, "Stop the Corrupt Courts."

As she pulled hard to open the big courthouse door, she couldn't help being amused, again, when she remembered what one of the judges had said when he first heard the "Free Homer" chant. "Why are they yelling, 'frijoles?'" the judge had wanted to know. "Frijoles is Spanish for 'beans.' I don't get it."

Someone had promptly told the judge that, No, it wasn't frijoles; it was "Free Homer." And had explained that a career criminal named Homer Harding had been convicted of capital murder for killing a police officer while under arrest for another murder. He had been sentenced to death. But crowds of people wanted Homer turned loose, claiming that he was innocent. None of these pro-Homer activists had any real information about the subject, but some folks just love an outlaw. So, people who felt inconsequential could get a sense of belonging by joining the "Free Homer" movement.

Maria settled down as she stepped into the elevator and pushed the button. At one of the floors for the District Attorney's office, she stepped out.

"Hello, Wendy," she said to the appellate section secretary, who occupied a desk in front near the elevators. Her desk held a large-print Bible and a copy of the Book of Mormon.

"Hi, Maria." Wendy Bachman was known throughout the office as "the Cussing Mormon" because of the odd combination of her raucous language and her religious practice.

"What's up?" Maria wanted to know.

"You have some sort of letter from the Fifth Circuit. The Court of Appeals. They must be setting the oral argument about that cop-killing rat-fucker. That Homer Harding guy."

"This court must be the only one left that doesn't rely just on email." Maria opened the envelope. "Yes. The Court of Appeals says the argument is set in July."

"I don't know the Homer Harding case very well, but what I heard was that this damn outlaw was a known police character. Arrested and in the police car. He'd been searched, but the search was piss poor. He still had a gun. And so this bastard turns sideways, even though he's handcuffed, and he shoots the officer in the front through the seat."

"That's exactly what the case is about. He didn't even try to escape. Cops all around."

"Okay, Maria. Get to work. You need to send this coward straight to hell."

"You mean I shouldn't listen to all that fine citizenry in front of the building, all yelling, 'Free Homer?'"

The Cussing Mormon laughed. "Fuck you, Maria."

"Now, Wendy, just listen to how you talk to your supervisor." Maria laughed too.

* * *

"Well, Jimmy, you're right about this borrowed servant idea."

"Of course I'm right." He said it with a smile.

Jennifer Lowenstein faced Jimmy again in his big corner office. Outside, the sun was in the west, and its light bounced off the grey and brown buildings to the south in flashes of gold. Tiny cars twenty floors below, in the late traffic, alternately shone in sunlight and crept into the shadows.

"We've put together a memorandum, but here's what it says." Jennifer looked through a wad of paper. "A person can be a borrowed servant of an employer other than his own, just the way you said, Jimmy. But the status of a borrowed servant isn't proved by just one factor. It's made up of a lot of factors that are listed in our memorandum."

"And as I recall, it's real, real confusing." Jimmy's smile got bigger.

"Yes. Everybody says that. It's hard to tell when your usual employer stops being your real employer and when you become the employee of another company, or when you become their so-called borrowed servant."

"That's good. We just have to get the jury to find that we borrowed everybody as our employees."

"The bottom line is what you said, Jimmy." Jennifer looked for the right page of the memorandum. "If you are the one who directs and controls the worker, that worker is your employee for purposes of worker's compensation. And that employee can't sue you. That employee is a borrowed servant, and he just gets the insurance—the worker's compensation insurance."

"Have you got court opinions that explain it?"

"Here's a good one. It's recent. 2014." Jennifer read the key words: "*Under the 'borrowed servant doctrine,' a worker in the general employ of one employer may become the borrowed servant of a second employer who controls the manner and details of the employee's work.*"

"Yeah. That's exactly what we want."

"That court granted summary judgment, saying that the worker was a borrowed servant and was limited to worker's compensation insurance. He couldn't sue for negligence-type damages."

"Just like we want to happen!" Jimmy's croak was higher pitched than usual. It was starting to sound like real excitement.

"That case was called *McQuagge v. Heil Trailer International Company*. But those names aren't important to remember, because it's cited in the memorandum."

"Okay."

"Here's another one. It says, '*No one factor is decisive, and no fixed test is used to determine the existence of a borrowed servant relationship.*'"

"That's good too. All we have to do is get the jury to say so, and the confusion will help us sell it to them."

"And this second case goes on to say, *"The fundamental question is whether someone has the power to control and direct another person in the performance of his work."*

"That's great! Emerald Petroleum had that power over everyone on the platform. Or, at least that's our version of the truth."

Jennifer knew what this terminology meant, just as she knew so many others of Jimmy's phraseologies.

Saying that this was "our version of the truth" meant that it might not be true at all. Or actually, it probably wasn't. But Jimmy Coleman was sure he could sell it to a jury.

12

wo days later, Jimmy Coleman once again found himself sitting at the desk with the red, brown, and green flowers. He
stared at the two pages that Jennifer Lowenstein had handed
to him.

"No, no, Jennifer. This isn't the way to write our answer."

He shook his head, but he wore a smile. For all of Jimmy's faults,
everybody in the firm knew that he was a wonderful teacher. Especially when instructing new lawyers about his own devious style.

"What did I do wrong?" Jennifer was puzzled. "Everything we discussed is in there, I think."

Jimmy fluttered the pages. "Not enough bulk to it."

"Not enough . . . bulk?"

"Length is a good thing in an answer. Or, for that matter, in a
complaint. Those kinds of court papers need to have bulk. Length.
Lots of variations. Lots of different material."

"Why is that, Jimmy?"

"Strategy. There actually are several reasons for it. First of all,
deny more stuff. Deny every factual allegation you possibly can. That
gives the plaintiff's lawyers more work to do. And it means more worry
for them. Also, it signals to them that we're going to defend this case
more vigorously than they might hope."

"Okay. But that's only a little piece of it, the denials."

"Well, but there's more. Drag out your affirmative defenses. State
and restate and restate them again, using different concepts and
different language. Of course, keep a paragraph for each type of defense that is global, too. A paragraph that states each one as broadly

and inclusively as possible. So that it covers everything possible about the particular defense in whatever situation develops at trial."

"All right, Jimmy." Jennifer smiled. "What is the strategy behind all of this, the strategy that I'm missing?"

"We are good jungle fighters, and we are creating a jungle." Jimmy's voice scratched as usual, and he laughed.

She laughed too. "And what is our objective with that? What do we gain by planting a jungle?"

"The ability to hide things. But hide them legally, I mean. Inscrutability and deception. An army at war always starts an invasion with a diversion, or a series of them. So can we. If we have an answer that raises a blizzard of defenses, it will make Robert Herrick spread his efforts out over all of them. That's the inscrutability.

"And also, we can make the case into a series of diversions by acting as though we're emphasizing defenses that we really don't think are going to work, while we're actually building up other defenses that we think will work. That's the deception. Except that it's a perfectly legal kind of deception. Just like military forces using a diversion."

"But won't Robert Herrick learn all about our case through the discovery process? I mean, through pretrial questioning and so forth?"

"He'll learn about the evidence. And you always learn that imperfectly. But the real point is about hiding the strategy. He won't learn our strategy through pretrial questioning of witnesses."

"True."

"So, you think you know what to do, now?"

She laughed again. "Makes perfect sense, Jimmy. I'm on it."

* * *

The former Miss Tamaulipas was naked as she rolled and cavorted on the big bed. Next to her was her younger sister. The women had not exactly consented to this activity, but they were at the service of the cartel leader. El Raton was next to the two of them, in similar undress, except that, being vain, he wore a T-shirt to cover his beer belly.

The location was an elegant room that was maintained in one of the cartel soldiers' homes not far from El Raton's own hacienda. The usual inhabitants of this house knew how to make themselves scarce whenever the place was needed by the Jefe—the Boss. El Raton was not greatly concerned about the possibility that his hideaway might become known to his wife, whom everyone called "Señora Raton," or "Mrs. Mouse." El Raton had no fear of stray gossip. No one would do that. If anyone did, the listener would be as likely as not to go tell El Raton, for the possibility of gaining his favor, and the gossiper would be dead.

Suddenly, outside the window, there was a long low whistle. It came from a loyal cartel soldier posted as a sentry. El Raton rolled off the bed and knelt by the window. He looked between the blinds.

"Jefe, I got a call." The sentry held a disposable telephone of the kind that El Raton brought into the compound by the truckload, because no one was allowed to use a phone for more than a few days. "The watchman at the hacienda says you got a message, Jefe. It has to do with something happening in the United States."

Griping and grumbling, El Raton dismissed the two ladies. He put on his clothes. And he trudged home, feeling unfulfilled and interrupted.

The six men who had visited him earlier were there in the great room. Like a Greek chorus, they started telling their story. One speaker at a time.

"Jefe, Boss," said the first voice, shakily, "we found out about the helicopter that called the Coast Guard to the Emerald Rose platform."

"And who flew the helicopter that lost us our goods," said the second voice.

Next, a third speaker. "The company is a charter service called Port Arthur Aviation. We found it on the internet. That company has dark red helicopters with 'Port Arthur Aviation' painted on the side."

And a fourth. "The best information we have is that the reason the helicopter was there was that the charter party wanted to investigate the Emerald Rose. To find out about the explosion there."

El Raton was impatient by now, because this was all proceeding too slowly. "Who was it that chartered the aircraft?" he demanded.

The fifth voice said, "Jefe, we do not know. We could not find that out."

"*Mierda!*" El Raton's curse echoed around in the hacienda. "*Idiotas!* I want that guy dead. And to get him to be dead, you've got to find out who he is."

"Si, Jefe."

"You morons interrupted me in an important meeting." El Raton was indignant. "Get out of here, and come back with something useful."

The Greek chorus shuffled out of the great room, and from there, out of the hacienda.

*   *   *

"We just got Jimmy Coleman's answer to our Emerald Rose lawsuit." Tom Kennedy walked into Robert's spacious office. "It's a real beauty. It's got defenses that most of us have never heard of, and it's nine pages long."

"We should have expected that. But it's okay. Sometimes, you can get a lot of mileage just by reading that kind of answer to the jury during your opening statement."

Outside, it was another rainy day, the kind of day that this city recently had suffered through too many times. The weather forecast had said that there would be flooding. "Don't drive into any underpasses," was the usual advice. "Leave work early if you can." Big buckets of water hit the floor-to-ceiling windows and shook them.

"There's a whole lot of denial, denial, denial in Jimmy's answer. Of course, he denies that Emerald Petroleum was negligent. Denies the facts about negligence. Denies that Emerald Rose was the proximate cause of any damages. Denies the damages, too."

"That's just Jimmy-Coleman-talk. You knew he'd say all of that."

"He says that the injured and dead, or some of them, were contributorily negligent."

"Not a very nice thing to say about people who are hurt." Robert pretended to a kind of shocked horror.

"And then, there's this thing about how they all were employees. And he says that means they can't recover anything but worker's compensation."

"Well, I suppose that's true of Emerald Petroleum's employees. But those plaintiffs can recover from the other companies. They have claims against Dalliman, particularly."

"You don't understand. Jimmy claims that *everybody there* was an employee of Emerald Petroleum."

"What?"

"It's that old 'borrowed servant' ripoff."

"But they weren't even close to being borrowed servants. Dalliman, for example, was completely independent. Their guys were there to operate and maintain their stuff. To deal with the Blowout Preventer and parts of the drill stem that Dalliman supplied. Those Dalliman guys weren't 'borrowed servants' of Emerald Petroleum. They had their own crew chief who told them what to do."

"Don't tell me. Tell Jimmy Coleman."

"Well, we'll have to file a reply to that borrowed servant garbage."

"And that's not the end of it. Jimmy has all kinds of references to different kinds of things that he claims were 'Acts of God.' Which he says Emerald had no reason to anticipate, and for which Emerald allegedly is not responsible. And separately from that, he says that the whole thing was an 'unavoidable accident.'"

"Those defenses don't fit, of course. But Jimmy threw them against the wall to see if they'd stick."

"He even pleads that the incident was *'force majeure.'*"

Robert started laughing. "That's not a defense to negligence. That's something you put into a contract."

"And then, Jimmy's answer blames everybody else. He says, 'In the extremely unlikely event that the jury should find Emerald Petroleum negligent, responsible, or liable, Emerald Petroleum pleads that the occurrence in question was proximately caused by the negligence of Dalliman Company, Momex Offshore, and the Amadanko Corporation.'"

"Well, but he has to plead that."

"Of course. But think about the implications."

"I already have." Robert laughed again. "I mean, I shouldn't laugh, but that's all you can do, given that it's Jimmy Coleman. A bunch of people dead, a bunch of people horribly injured, and Jimmy comes up with all this word salad."

"What I mean, Robert, is this. Consider the worst case scenario. The worst case, depending on what the jury finds. I mean, short of the jury saying that no one was hurt and no one was careless."

"I've already thought about the worst case. Imagine that the jury buys this 'borrowed servant' garbage. That means we can't recover anything from Emerald Petroleum. And suppose that the jury also finds that Emerald Petroleum was the one with the most fault. Suppose they say Emerald was ninety percent at fault. Then, our plaintiffs can only recover ten percent of their damages from Dalliman, Momex, and Amadanko. A hundred thousand dollars suddenly becomes ten thousand, and a million dollars gets cut down the same way."

"Right." Tom sat down, heavily.

Robert looked out at the driving rain. "If anyone thought this was going to be an easy case, they sure were wrong."

13

What's happened to the derrick?" Tom Kennedy pointed at the video image of the burning Emerald Rose. "Usually there's a derrick at the top of an oil well."

"A lot of that stuff melted," Johnny Tull explained. "It collapsed or got blown off the platform."

They sat in the conference room at the offices of Robert Herrick and Associates. Instead of the brilliant day outside, all that could be seen was the curtain that covered the floor-to-ceiling windows. Everyone's eyes were on the big screen at the front of the room that showed images of the Emerald Rose. Leaning, blackened, and burning.

"You're the expert, Johnny," Tom acknowledged. "But wow. The steel melted?"

"Yes. The heat's that intense."

Tom and Robert, along with several associates and Johnny, were watching a film that showed plumes of fire erupting from the Emerald Rose. Above the fragments of the platform, three tongues of orange flared from a central core of flame. "The flames rise up over two hundred and fifty feet into the air," Johnny said.

He pointed. "These are flares from methane and all kinds of other hydrocarbon gases. And also, hydrogen sulfide, H_2S. Which is highly toxic. In a way, it's a good thing it's burning, because hydrogen sulfide will kill you. Although the sulfur dioxide that results from combustion is bad too if you breathe it."

Robert frowned. "Must be dangerous as all get out to be anywhere near there."

"Absolutely. These firefighters are going to use brass tools, for instance. Brass doesn't make a spark. Doesn't matter now, because there's already a pretty big spark."

"Yes." Everyone chuckled at that understatement.

"But sparks matter when the fire is extinguished, before they can cap the well. A spark then would be disastrous. See the fireboats pumping wet stuff on the fire now?"

"What is it they're spraying?"

"Nothing sophisticated." Johnny Tull smiled. "Just sea water. They'll hose up a lot of water, and they have plenty of that."

"And I guess they'll set off an explosion right above the well," Robert said. "I read up on this. An explosion can put out the fire, because it removes the oxygen, just like blowing out a candle. Explosions are the standard method of oil well firefighting."

"Well . . . no." Johnny smiled again. "That was the old way. Today, nobody puts out oil well fires with explosions. Just watch and see what they do."

"I'm behind the times, as usual." Robert laughed.

The film showed a white screen momentarily, and then it jumped.

"Okay, this film is edited," Johnny said, as the scene changed. "We have the whole film, but there are hours where nothing happens. Now, you can see that they've built a temporary working deck so they can set up a jet cutter. It has nozzles that spray sand and water fast enough to make a clean horizontal cut across the pipe."

A big vessel was stationed near the platform, now. "That's the crane barge. See what it's got on the crane, on the end of that long boom?"

Robert stared. "Just looks like a piece of pipe to me."

"It's called a Venturi tube. The well control guys place it over the wellhead to divert the flame so they can work at close quarters. It protects against the scorching radiant heat. And now, they're lifting the jet cutter onto the deck."

"I hope these guys are well paid."

"Oh, my, yes. They are."

Everybody watched as the jet cutter worked, steadily carving into the steel of the wellhead. The damaged pipe fell away. The tongues of fire merged into one enormous flare, which soared three hundred feet over the Venturi tube.

"Now, they'll install a custom-built Blowout Preventer and get ready to close the valves."

Everybody watched with renewed expectation while sea water sprayed and flames burst from the Venturi tube like an inverted rocket. But suddenly . . . , the room went dark, the fire disappeared, and the noise stopped booming.

"Just like that?" Robert was incredulous.

"Well, yes and no. There's a lot more to it. They've got to divert the flow into a pipeline, because the pressures are just too great."

"And I guess that does it?"

"That does it for the hard part. They'll have to kill the well by pumping in heavy fluid, and they'll drill another well so that they can cement this one."

"Well, as I was saying," Robert spoke quietly. "I hope they're well paid."

* * *

That evening, once again, Robert steered his car into the entrance beside the green sign with the golden sun. The sign that said, Sunrise Green Assisted Living.

He made his way down the corridor, trying to ignore the smell of medicine and death.

"Hi, Mama."

"Oh! It's so good to see you. But call me Rosalie, please. Calling me Mama makes me feel old."

". . . All right. . . . Ahhh . . . Rosalie." Strange. But if it made her feel better, okay.

"Have you been practicing law today?"

"Yes, Mama. Uh, Rosalie."

"Is it fun? You do better if you decide that it's fun."

"Yes. That's true, of course."

"And if you run into disagreeable people, always remember that they are fun too. You can learn something from anyone, no matter how disagreeable." She laughed.

That made him marvel at how she could tell the truth about a profession she didn't know. It was almost as though she had practiced law herself.

Suddenly, he saw something on the wall that made him very angry. Something that didn't belong there at all. He tried to keep his feelings quiet. But he wound up cutting the visit short, and out in the hall, he asked for the manager.

"Look. I want that calendar in my mother's room removed, right now! What is a calendar doing in my mother's room, a calendar that comes from the Clark-Benning Funeral Home? From a mortuary? Get it out of there right away. I mean, now."

"Ahhh ... yes sir. Most people want a calendar. But certainly, I'll take it away."

"What's that thing there for? Are you trying to drum up business for the Clark-Benning Funeral Home?" He was getting angrier and angrier. "You want to refer her to them, and you get a kickback or something?"

That remark was out of line, he thought to himself as he drove home. Quarrels in the courthouse lead to quarrels in personal business, because it's hard for a lawyer to turn off the adversary mindset. Especially when that lawyer thinks about an adversary like Jimmy Coleman.

* * *

The next morning, across town, the same group of lawyers who had watched the Emerald Rose film gathered in a big room with folding chairs.

"Welcome to our Demonstration Center," said a man in a dark blue suit. "I'm Derek Zender, and I'm from Data Analysis Corporation, which is your host right now."

"We're proud to be here, Derek." Robert Herrick spread his arm to point around the big room. "And these folks are our team for the Emerald Rose litigation."

He faced the group. "Lawyers, I want you all to know what we're doing next in our case. We're going to have literally millions of documents from the defendants. We can't read them all. That's where Derek and Data Analysis Corporation come in. We've hired them to search the documents electronically."

"That's right," said Derek Zender. "We specialize in electronic searches of records. We've studied how to generate search terms for a given case, and we have proprietary software to do it."

He gestured toward a screen, which had "Data Analysis Corporation" written on it, together with a logo using a stylized version of the letters "DAC." The lights dimmed.

"Our job is part art, part science." Derek Zender changed the screen. "A search has to be based on words. We look for documents that contain key words. The key words can't be excessively common in the documents, because then, we'd flag nearly every document, and you'd still have too many to read. And our search can't be too narrow, because then we'd miss crucial documents."

Robert nodded. "What we want Derek to do, of course, is to find documents that help us present our case. Documents that show how the defendants were at fault. We also want documents that will help the defendants, too, so that we can anticipate them at trial."

"Right." The man in the blue suit changed the screen. "So we at Data Analysis have considered the case, studied random documents, and figured out search terms. For instance, when we identified all documents containing the term, 'Blowout Preventer,' the system returned way too many documents."

The screen changed again. "We experimented, and we found that instead, if we used the phrase 'Blowout Preventer' and plus, we also required 'blowout' and 'failure' or any of several other terms in the same sentence, we got reasonable quantities of documents, and we were statistically likely to find the relevant ones. Our software lets us do that kind of search."

Another screen change. "And that's just one example. Here are some others." Derek Zender explained the rest of his search efforts.

Finally, the screen showed the logo and the name of Data Analysis Corporation again. And the lights in the room brightened.

"Okay, that's it," said Robert. "We'll let Derek complete his job. And then, there's good news and bad news. The good news is that we think Derek is well on the way toward getting us a manageable number of documents and flagging the important ones."

He grinned. "But the bad news is this. When the best documents are identified, we have to evaluate them the old-fashioned way."

"What's that?" asked a new associate. "What's the old fashioned way?"

Robert chuckled. "That's when we've got to do something very painful. Namely . . . we have to read 'em all."

14

Mr. Westhoven, you're what we call the lead plaintiff," Robert said to the man sitting across from him, beside Tom Kennedy.

"I'm the what?" Mr. Westhoven wore a dark gray suit and a light blue tie, and he had a brilliant smile. An attractive appearance was a desirable attribute in a lead plaintiff.

The day outside was filled with sunshine. Along Buffalo Bayou, the grass was a glittering green ribbon. Beneath the three men, the huge oriental carpet showed its many colors more brightly than usual.

"You're the lead plaintiff. You're the one we're going to want to feature in the courtroom most prominently. By the way, call me Robert. Is it okay if I call you Randall?"

"Randy." The lead plaintiff grinned.

"Okay. It's Randy. Well, we have your name first among the list of plaintiffs on our suit papers. We picked you out because you make a good impression. You'll end up testifying the most, for instance."

"Thanks. I guess. I don't know if I like that. But okay. I want to follow what my lawyer says."

"And thanks for that. Now, Randy, we are getting into the part of the lawsuit called 'discovery.' There is a discovery period, a time period, for most lawsuits in this particular court."

"I know a little bit about that. Discovery. My company has been in a few lawsuits that I've had to follow, unfortunately. Discovery is about finding out the evidence that the other side has."

"Right. And it usually proceeds in a certain order. It starts with each side having to give particular kinds of information to the other.

We've done all of that. Then we usually use what are called 'interrogatories.'"

"And those are . . . ?"

"They're written questions that follow up on the information we get earlier. Mostly, in this case, to identify documents. And then, the third stage is that we request the other side's documents."

"I've been through that. What a mess."

"Well, we're in the middle of that right now. We have more than three million documents to go through."

"Three million? You must have a huge warehouse."

"Yes, in a way. It's called a computer memory. Most of the documents are electronic."

"So, how can you possibly read three million documents?"

"We don't. We've hired an outside company that has expertise in electronic searches. There will also be some paper documents, and the search company will scan those in searchable form."

"Wow."

"And the search will identify the important documents. And then, those documents will still be many thousands, and so they'll go through another search that will prioritize them."

"I got it." Randy Westhoven nodded.

"Well, but the next step after that is what are called depositions. And we are starting to schedule those now."

"Remind me—?"

"Depositions just mean that we ask questions of the other side's witnesses, and they ask our witnesses. In front of a court reporter, who takes it all down. Usually, right here in the office, instead of a courtroom. So, the other side's lawyers, including Jimmy Coleman, might be asking our experts and our witnesses questions, and I have a right to be there, and our lawyers, including me, will be asking their witnesses questions."

"And, like, who will be the witnesses?"

"The various expert witnesses we've hired, including some we still have to find and hire. The survivors who were on the platform, who lived through the explosion. The executives and supervisors in the companies we've sued. And there's one other important group."

"Who's that?"

"The actual plaintiffs. Like you. You're the lead plaintiff. Number one."

"Oh." Randy Westhoven's smile disappeared for a moment. "I . . . I guess so."

* * *

The assistant DA looked at the file for a moment. "Pepper Herrick. Real name is Cynthia Herrick. The charge . . . well, it's intoxication assault. And I see from her rap sheet, she has a prior. An earlier DWI."

Pepper's lawyer stood to the side and looked at the police report. "But I can tell you, it's not really an intoxication assault. What I mean is, it can't be proved as an intoxication assault in a trial."

"Why's that?" The assistant DA smiled, because he had heard a lot of defense stories that hadn't proved to be accurate. But then again, like all prosecutors, he'd seen a few of these sob stories turn out to be true. So, like all prosecutors, he had to listen, even if he was skeptical.

The two lawyers talked inside the Criminal Justice Center, which was a twenty-story high-rise building. Pepper sat in the audience area of the courtroom on one of the dark wooden benches, with her husband Jonathan beside her. Her lawyer and the assistant DA stood by the counsel table near the judge's bench, which was unoccupied during this plea bargaining time. A dozen lawyers and prosecutors milled around them.

"That isn't just my take on it." Pepper's lawyer was deferential. "You'll want to check it out. But it starts with the law. It can't be intoxication assault unless the injury is really, really bad. The law says that the victim has to suffer the loss of a 'bodily member or organ' before it can be intoxication assault."

"Okay. I'm with you. Except, it also says 'protracted loss of use' of that bodily member or organ. That's enough to make it intoxication assault, losing the use of a body part for a long time."

The assistant DA happened to be a tall black man with a trimmed beard, a tan suit, and a forest green tie. His shirt was a white button-down, and his legs and arms were agile, which put a faint touch of two-step into his stance. Pepper's lawyer had the frame of a prize fighter. He covered it with the lawyer's uniform: a dark pinstriped suit and a red tie. He also wore a gold stud earring, which he removed, it was said, whenever he was in front of a jury.

"And okay, I'm with you too." Pepper's lawyer smiled. "If someone loses a leg from the accident, or loses the use of that leg for a *'protracted'* period—whatever that means—well, that can be intoxication assault."

"Or loses a tooth."

"Maybe. But here's my point. The injury in this case wasn't much of an injury. It was only a hairline crack in one of the bones of the foot. The guy got out of the hospital the next day. He had a walking cast for a short while. He didn't lose anything for any sort of 'protracted' time, whatever that means."

The assistant DA laughed. "Why do you reckon they use words like 'protracted'?"

"You got me. All I know is that we had to use what they called a 'protractor' in high school geometry class. As to why, I never had a clue."

The two sometimes-adversaries both laughed. Every lawyer has to marvel, now and then, at how pompous the words of the law can be. Maybe these majestic sounds are designed to seem pompous, so that they can make the law come off as just that: majestic.

"All right." The prosecutor sounded amused and philosophical, both at the same time. "You've got my attention."

Sometimes the excuses are true, and assistant DA's are like everyone else. They don't usually have death wishes, and they don't want to discover that the defense story is the correct one in the middle of a trial.

"So, that's my argument." Pepper's lawyer spread his hands. "As for the question whether she was intoxicated . . . , well, she doesn't have the stomach to fight it. Unless, that is, you decided to make us, and then we would have to fight. But if it's only a DWI and she pleads, what can you do?"

"I've got to check it all out. But if you're right, it's probably just a repeat-type driving while intoxicated case. I usually want thirty days on a second DWI."

"Yeah, but you can do a lot better than that. The Penal Code might even let you recommend a sentence of probation for the thirty days."

"I can't do that, of course. But let me check out this guy with the injury."

"Yeah. And how about, maybe, see if the jail time can get a little more merciful. A little more reasonable. I mean, *thirty days in the County Jail?*" Pepper's lawyer gagged. "You might as well be sentenced to life in prison."

He drew another laugh from the prosecutor, along with a nod of the head.

* * *

Across town, Jennifer Lowenstein sat across from Jimmy Coleman in front of the Italian intarsiato chest.

"It really isn't fair. I guess it never is."

"Yes." Jimmy was philosophical. "We have to spend a hundred thousand or more to produce documents. And we have to be thorough. Nowadays, if you try to bury documents, electronic specialists can tell."

"But the other side, the plaintiffs—they don't have very many documents."

"We've written a pretty stout document request for Herrick, but you're right. They've already gathered all the health care records. Those will tell us only a little. We'll have to get comprehensive records from their doctors and so forth. And it's not really very likely that we'll get much about the explosion itself from these plaintiffs. Maybe so, if they wrote something about it, such as in an insurance application that describes the accident. But that's unlikely to help us very much."

"It's unfair. Like I say." She smiled. "But I guess we're used to it."

"Well, there's one place where we'll get a lot of documents. So many that we'll have to hire them out to be searched by computer specialists."

"What's that?"

"The other companies who are sued as defendants. Remember, the defendants are all going to be pointing the finger at each other. And so, we'll get millions of documents from Dalliman, Momex Offshore, and Amadanko."

"Oh. Sure."

"And we've already requested those, and they've started to come in. We already have our discovery responses for those companies done, because it's basically the same as for Robert Herrick and the plaintiffs."

"But there's one more unfair thing."

"What's that?" Jimmy looked up.

"Reading all those documents after the electronic guys do their search. I have to read them," Jennifer complained. "And I can delegate to a bunch of first- and second-year associates, but you know how it is, Jimmy. I'll have to do a lot of it myself, until these furshlugginer documents are coming out my ears."

15

Port Arthur Aviation." The receptionist announced the name just as she had been taught, with happy friendliness. With a smile in her voice.

"Hello, Port Arthur Aviation," a voice said. "I'd like to rent a helicopter. Can you give me the reservations department, please?"

"Sure." The receptionist did not take particular notice of the origin of the call, which was Tamaulipas State, in Mexico. The English spoken by the voice was perfect and unaccented.

A pause. Then: "Charter operations. This is Billy."

The voice spoke promptly. "As I told the receptionist, I'd like to rent a helicopter. Preferably a Sikorsky, like maybe an S-62. Can you help me with that?"

"I can totally help you with that."

"Good."

"In fact, I can even give you a special. We don't actually run specials, but we have an S-62 with the rental reduced during the last week of August. Business is slow at that time, for some unknown reason."

"Okay, great. Any day that week will do."

"Name and address?"

"You already have it," said the voice confidently. "We rented the same aircraft recently on June 27 this year. If you can look that up, it'll make things easy."

"Okay. Gimme just a minute."

"Sure."

A pause. ". . . Okay. Here it is . . . . Tom Kennedy, right?"

"Yes. I'm calling for him."

"Tom Kennedy, at Robert Herrick and Associates. Got it. Top floor, Chase Tower. Zip is 77002. Is that correct?"

"Yes. All correct."

"It's a law firm."

"Right. A law firm." This was news to the voice, but he was prepared to sound confident.

"Okay. I'll just transfer all this information to your date. Ahhh . . . what date do you want in that week?"

"Any date is actually okay. Let's just say . . . Tuesday."

"Okay . . . ."

And after a few finalities and goodbyes, the voice hung up.

Now, the information that El Raton wanted would be available to him. The flight of that Sikorsky had been directed by someone named Tom Kennedy. Who was at the top floor of the Chase Tower.

Now, El Raton would know who to retaliate against for messing with his business. And the man behind the voice knew that in one way or another, he would be rewarded.

* * *

Meanwhile, several hundred miles to the north, Tom Kennedy sat in front of Robert's desk. He looked to the west, through the greenhouse windows and toward the horizon.

"This next month is going to be a marathon," he said.

"No kidding. At least twenty depositions on each side."

"Jimmy's going at it in a really strange way, by taking the plaintiffs themselves first. He wants to take the depositions, first, of the family members who are suing for the deaths of their relatives. I can't figure it."

"Me neither. I guess he's hoping to soften them up."

"Maybe. Or to catch some kind of contradiction. But I can't see what it would be."

"Well, we'll produce Randy Westhoven first. Our lead plaintiff. He's a strong individual, and he can stand it."

"Right. But then what?"

"Eventually, the defendants are going to want to take depositions from all of the plaintiffs. After the first ones, we can hope they'll be short."

"Well, we've got to figure out how we're going to do our depositions. I'd say the first thing would be the head guy who was on the platform for Emerald Petroleum. They actually had a VP there."

"But he's not going to know a lot that's technical. He was a VP of personnel and was there just to celebrate the well reaching depth."

"That may turn out to be even better, I'm guessing. We'll get from him a description of what happened. He'll be prepared by Jimmy to give us the least amount of information possible, of course. But whatever he does give, it will be valuable, because it comes from a big guy within Emerald. Even if it's not technical. It can contradict their experts, if they vary from the truth."

"What then?"

"Then, we take depositions of workers who were there on the platform. And supervisors. Let's get a representative group from all the defendants. Then, executives. Then, we'll take their outside expert witnesses."

"It's a big job."

"It's a big case."

* * *

"May it please the court." Maria Melendes started with the customary introduction.

"Ms. Melendes."

But she was not actually in a courtroom. The setting was the District Attorney's office. This was a moot court—a simulation—and the three "judges" were other assistant district attorneys, sitting behind a library table. Maria usually did this sort of practice run right before an argument in the Court of Appeals.

And this case was important to Maria. The convicted man, sentenced to death, was Homer Harding. He was the man who, while handcuffed and under arrest for murder, had murdered one of the arresting officers. His sentence had been affirmed by several loops through the courts, and now he was appealing in the federal system.

Homer Harding was also the man who was the subject of so many well-attended protests. The counterculture placard carriers didn't know the case against him at all, but they were certain that their guy was innocent. In fact, Maria had seen a few "Free Homer" protesters today, when she had entered the building. Only a few, because nothing official was scheduled for Homer Harding today, but the fact that he had any supporters at all was a tribute to the man's fame. He was a genuine criminal hero.

"Homer Harding's first argument is so-called 'actual innocence,'" Maria began. "We disagree with that, completely. We know, of course, that the Supreme Court has said that a new showing of 'actual innocence' requires a new evidence hearing. Well, this is a long way from that."

One of the pretend judges interrupted. "But Ms. Melendes, the petitioner doesn't claim actual innocence. He just claims he wasn't legally subject to the death penalty."

"Yes, your honor. The argument is usually referred to as 'actual innocence of the death penalty.' That's a strange phrase, I'll admit. In essence, the defendant is saying, 'maybe I'm guilty of just plain murder, yes, but I'm not guilty of capital murder. The kind that qualifies for the death penalty.' In other words, he's claiming 'actual innocence of the death penalty.'"

"Okay. But hasn't he made a showing of that on this appeal, so that an evidentiary hearing is necessary?"

"No, your honor. The defendant's argument is that he didn't intend to discharge the gun that he had hidden in his pants. It just happened to go off and kill the police officer who was driving the car. But that argument isn't based on new evidence, and in fact it was fully presented at the trial. And it was rejected by the jury.

"And by the way, your honors, that 'accident' argument was unbelievable. I've got to brag on the petitioner's lawyers for thinking this one up. They're saying, while Homer Harding was handcuffed, he got his gun out of his pants somehow, and he just happened to turn sideways, and it just happened to point itself frontward, and then the gun just happened to discharge, completely by accident, and it just happened to kill the police officer. And I guess that accidental shot must have been real, real accurate."

The pretend judges smiled. "Well, but the issue isn't whether we believe the petitioner's claim. This is the appeals court, not the jury."

"No. That's right. But the real point is that the rule of actual innocence only applies to something new, and this story already has been raised at the trial. The jury rejected it, and they should have rejected it, because it isn't credible at all." She paused. "And now, I'd like to get into the petitioner's other arguments."

The moot court lasted for two more hours, much longer than the argument before the real judges would be. But for Maria, the purpose was to raise as many questions as possible, so that she would be prepared to answer even the unusual ones.

16

Jimmy Coleman wore the face of a British bulldog. His angriest look, for this deposition.

"Randall Westhoven," he croaked, "you have produced certain materials to us, which are now marked as Exhibit 1 to your deposition. And you've been sworn, so let me ask you this. These items in Exhibit 1, these are absolutely all of the photographs and writings that you have in your possession from your father, is that right?"

"Yes, sir," answered the lead plaintiff. He had a strained look on his face. Very few plaintiffs are comfortable having their depositions taken, and Jimmy Coleman knew how to exploit their feelings.

"There's not much in Exhibit 1 to back up your claims, is there, Randall Westhoven?"

"It's not much of my daddy, no. I wish I had more of him. But he's gone, along with the Emerald Rose, and all I have is this . . . stuff."

Questioning witnesses in depositions is very different from questioning them at trial. In a deposition, you're finding things out. It's a glorified interview, even if it's on the record. You don't have to worry about what the jury thinks. Not yet. All you want is for the witness to say things that can help you when you do go to trial.

Jimmy Coleman was a master at it.

Here in Robert Herrick's conference room, Jimmy sat in a heavy heap beside the court reporter. He wore an obviously expensive, but still ill-fitting, ice blue suit. And a wildly colored tie that sported a lot of red. Around the big mahogany table, there were a half dozen black-suited Booker and Bayne associates, who were all unnecessary here.

Jimmy always brought a posse, even if his hangers-on didn't do any-thing.

"Now, Randall Westhoven," Jimmy grated, "I see in your Com-plaint, in your suit papers, that you claim you've lost the companion-ship and solace of your father."

"That's . . . right."

"But there's nothing in these pictures and writings in Exhibit 1 that refers to any activity that you and your father did together for companionship. Isn't that right?"

A pause. "I . . . guess that's right."

Randy Westhoven, the lead plaintiff, was well dressed, as Robert expected him to be, in a grey suit and maroon tie. Robert watched his face. Behind his rimless glasses, the man obviously was pained by this. He had described himself as twenty-eight years old and his father as fifty. Even that factual statement was hard for him.

Jimmy didn't react to the distress of the man he was questioning. "And, Randall Westhoven, I see that your lawyers claim you lost the value of your father's advice and guidance, too. That's what they claim, don't they?"

"I guess . . . so. I don't recall the exact words."

"But there's not a single thing in Exhibit 1 that involves your father giving you advice and guidance, is there?"

"Ahhh . . . no. But he did."

"You're an investment adviser, aren't you, Randall Westhoven? You're good at telling people what stocks they should buy or sell?"

"I'm an investment adviser, yes. I usually leave it to my clients to decide whether I'm good at it."

"Your father was a supervisor on offshore oil platforms?"

"Yes."

"Your father couldn't very well give you guidance about invest-ments, the thing you spend the largest part of your time with?"

"Ahhh . . . no."

"And it's not entirely clear from this Complaint, Randall Westho-ven, but I gather you're asking for a large amount of money. In the five-to-ten-million-dollar range. Right?"

"That is up to the lawyers."

"If someone had five million dollars and put it in tax-free bonds, they'd earn enough every year for their family to live well for the rest of their life, wouldn't they? Just from that?"

"I guess so. . . . I guess . . . ."

Randy Westhoven's eyes were wet. Robert stared at him. One of the hardest things to do, as a plaintiff's lawyer, is to prepare your client to testify and then watch him do it. It is like watching from afar while a child, whom you've taught to do a relatively complex task, tries to perform that task. You stare at every step, and you share every inch of the child's uncertainty and anxiety. You want to help.

But you can't.

The trouble was, there was nothing improper about Jimmy's questions. Robert was waiting for him to ask something like, "You want to exchange your father's life for those tax-free bonds, don't you?" And then he would object. But Jimmy didn't.

What Jimmy did, instead, was to keep Randall Westhoven answering questions for nearly four hours. His questions were proper under the rules, but they were also cruel and tasteless.

* * *

Back in the mountains of Tamaulipas State, El Raton finally could be enthusiastic with his cartel soldiers.

"Finally! We finally have some useful information."

"Yes, Jefe." "Yes, Jefe." The group of men assembled in the great room of the hacienda all said it more or less in unison.

"I'm a businessman, don't you see." El Raton beamed. "We're all businessmen. You're businessmen too. And this is a very competitive business. If you slack off at all, other people are going to take you over. You have to retaliate if someone interrupts your supply chain."

"Yes, Jefe." "Yes, Jefe."

"You see, we think in business terms. The kind they teach in business school. Our distribution method wasn't just a haphazard trip to that Emerald Rose Platform slapped together with a trip on another vessel to the States. That was our supply chain. Planned, and planned carefully. They teach about supply chains in business schools. I want us to have an efficient supply chain."

"Yes, Jefe." "Yes, Jefe."

"But if you are a businessman, you also have to be adaptable. You have to use methods that are fitted to the type of business you're in. And to the situation you face. A business like ours can't use exactly the same methods as other businesses. It's a matter of adaptation. In business school, they call this 'Contingency Theory.' In other words, our methods are contingent on the circumstances. 'Contingency Theory.' In our dynamic business, we can't use the same methods they use in stodgy industries like railroads or steel production."

"Yes, Jefe." "Yes, Jefe."

"I'm self-taught about these management techniques, as you know." El Raton waved his arms. He felt dominant, fulfilled, and altruistic. "I couldn't go to a normal business school in the United States, of course. Like the Harvard Business School, for instance. There are some things I can't do, in my position. So I studied up by using the internet. I studied management methods by using the internet."

"Yes, Jefe." "Yes, Jefe."

"And so our valued supply chain must be protected. By methods contingent on our industry and our type of business. We have a serious problem, and it calls for a sophisticated response."

"How, Jefe?" "What kind of sophisticated response, Jefe?"

"We kill 'em." El Raton was enjoying this immensely, and he laughed.

"How, Jefe?" "What sophisticated business method do we use to kill them, Jefe?"

"If I could, I'd like to make this particular Gringo into *guiso*. Stew. Inside a fifty-five gallon drum. That would go a long way toward discouraging other people from making trouble. But in this case, the target is a long way away. And he's in another country, where our control of things is not so decisive."

El Raton gestured with his hand to signal the finality of his decision. "We'll just have to do it however we can. By methods adapted to the circumstances. Our methods will have to be contingent on the situation. As in . . . , Contingency Theory. Maybe we will have to do something simple. Like, maybe, shoot the guy."

* * *

Meanwhile, Robert Herrick drove home in the dark. He was depressed about the deposition of Randy Westhoven that Jimmy Coleman had taken.

It wasn't that Randy had done poorly. He would make an excellent witness at trial, and the tricks and traps that Jimmy had used wouldn't really help the defense much. They might make Randy and other plaintiffs sick of the abuse and willing to settle for less, and maybe this was the purpose. But Robert thought the pain Jimmy had inflicted on Randy was unnecessary, and he disliked a system where tactics like this could work.

"Maria?" he called, as soon as he walked into the back door of his big home on Willowick Drive in River Oaks.

She didn't answer. Louder, he called, "Maria?"

Finally: "I'm here. But I'm hiding."

Her voice was bouncy. Not depressed, at all.

He laughed. "Okay. Where are you hiding?" He thought, maybe, he knew.

"In the bedroom."

He put on a silly voice. "And what do you suggest I do?"

"I suggest, dummy, that you come on up. I'm not wearing anything but a T-shirt."

"You've done that before. Maybe, something new?"

"Of course there's something new. The T-shirt is soaking wet."

By now he was at the top of the stairs. And in the bedroom. She jumped on him from the side, put her arms around his neck, and dumped water over his suit.

"Now, let me get this off," she said. She peeled away his jacket. His tie and shirt. Unbuckled his belt. And unreeled the zipper. Somehow, she already had his shoes off.

She knelt. And with her tongue circling him, she felt him grow.

So far, he had stood there still. Now, he ripped off her T-shirt and tore one of the arm openings. He lifted her and flopped her on her back on the bed.

She laughed. And dramatically, she blurted, "Have your way with me, Baby." She said it just for fun.

Minutes later, she started panting, with shrill little cries. The sound grew louder as she rose and rose in pain and joy until she couldn't hold it any longer. And neither could he.

Afterwards, he lay on his back, and she lay on top of him, with her chest against his.

He realized that he wasn't depressed any more.

Happy wife, happy life. Just as they say.

17

Francel Williams's office was tastefully understated. Tan walls with white trim, topped by substantial white crown molding. Chairs with Lincoln green upholstery that set off dark brown furniture. Sepia photographs that showed Francel in great moments, such as his being sworn in, years ago, as the county's first black man to become a court of appeals judge.

As usual, Francel was here wearing his trademark: a pinstriped charcoal suit with a silver tie. He sat at his conference table next to a court reporter. Across from him, there was a bald-headed man wearing a beard, a blue work shirt, and jeans.

"So, Mr. Dunkelman," Francel was saying, "what were your duties as a tool pusher on the Emerald Rose platform?"

"The tool pusher is the traditional name given to a drilling foreman, either onshore or off," the man answered. "And I was one of several of those on this platform, for different shifts."

Today marked the beginning of the plaintiff's depositions of the on-the-deck workers. There were so many that the lawyers were using a platoon system. Robert Herrick was asking questions of an Emerald vice president in another conference room across town. Tom Kennedy was at Jimmy Coleman's office, questioning a roughneck.

Francel continued his questioning. "How many years did you work as a tool pusher, Mr. Dunkelman, and what are your qualifications? What makes you an expert at that?"

The question was deliberately worded so that it would enable the plaintiffs to question this man at trial and ask for expert opinions.

"I've been an oilfield worker for more than twenty-five years. A tool pusher for more than ten. I don't have a lot of continuing education in a classroom, but I even have some of that. And I have plenty of education from the school of hard knocks. I have to know what will be cost-effective in exploring for oil and gas in all kinds of situations. I have to know what's safe and what's dangerous. And I have to be able to manage people."

Good. Now Francel was ready to get right to the point.

"Mr. Dunkelman, let me direct your attention to the decision to inject salt water to replace drilling mud in the Emerald Rose well. The VP of Production made that decision, I believe."

"That's right. It wasn't my decision, for sure."

"Where was that VP at this time?"

"In Port Arthur. On solid, safe dry land."

"And you disagreed with him, Mr. Dunkelman?"

"Yes. Definitely."

"What did you say to him?"

"I got him on the phone. And I told him, it wasn't a good idea. The mud was heavy. That's what was holding down the pressure at the bottom. The sea water was light."

"Were you yelling at him?"

"I . . . I guess so."

"And he answered you . . . , with what?"

"Something like, . . . well, that was the point. The sea water was lighter and would help us complete the well. And he was also concerned about the mud settling, which makes it hard to get out. But mostly it was a financial decision, for him. We were behind schedule. Way behind. And delay is money."

"You talked to him several times, I guess, to tell him what you thought?"

"I called him several times and told him over and over what a bad idea I thought it was."

"And that was what was done, injecting sea water to replace the mud? To lighten the force holding the pressure?"

"Yes. I had to do what he told me."

Now, Francel went for all the marbles. Cause and negligence. Conclusions from the tool pusher about the ultimate legal issues.

"And injecting sea water was what caused the blowout, right?"

The witness squirmed. "I can't say that. I just ... can't ... say that."

"Are you reluctant to speak out against your employer? Against Emerald Petroleum?"

"Yes, I am. You bet."

"If someone else said the sea water was what caused the blowout, you couldn't disagree with them, could you?"

A pause. "I guess not."

"And the reason you disagreed with the VP of Production about injecting sea water, was because you knew—from experience—that it wasn't safe, it wasn't prudent, and it wasn't what a reasonable person would do?"

"Well .... Yes."

Francel questioned the tool pusher for three hours, going over other issues. The failure of the Blowout Preventer. The sequence of events in the explosion. And so forth.

But Francel knew, with the admissions he had gotten from Mr. Dunkelman about his disagreements with the VP, he already had what was needed. He had gotten an expert opinion from inside the company, confirming Emerald Petroleum's liability.

* * *

Through the huge window in El Raton's great room, you could see row upon row of Sierra Madre ranges. They were green and faded to gray in the distance, under the Tamaulipas sun.

Today was a good day. El Raton had discovered a new supply chain. A vessel, which would change each time, would sail from a Tamaulipas harbor, which would also change each time, and rendezvous with a helicopter from Louisiana. Which changed periodically, and so did its point of embarkation.

The method was a little more expensive, but it worked.

Now, El Raton sat in his great room with his first lieutenant, a big man named Charro. The two businessmen drank tequila martinis made with a recipe that El Raton had invented.

"Now that our supply chain is working again, Charro, maybe we can to shift over to a Just-in-Time business model." El Raton said it with a contented smile.

"How do we do that, Jefe?" Charro was a little timid about admitting he didn't knowing much business-school stuff.

"It means you only perform tasks that are immediately needed. Instead of having our inventory of merchandise, we would get each kilo just when we needed it. Just in Time. It saves you from having to finance a lot of inventory. You keep a little inventory, but only a little."

"It sounds brilliant."

El Raton was excited now. "And you only transport it as needed. Just in Time."

"Won't that be hard for us to do?"

"Maybe. They say businesses that adopt Just-in-Time methods need to be agile. Nimble. They have to be able to move quickly to adjust inventory if they don't keep much of it."

"Right. I see."

"That's one of the reasons, besides good advertising, for the success of Federal Express. FedEx. They've sold businesses on the idea of Just-in-Time management, because they can supply stores and factories overnight."

Charro chuckled. "Maybe we can use FedEx."

"And then, we ought to hire their advertising company, too." El Raton laughed.

"Speaking of time, Jefe," Charro asked, "isn't it time for us to think about getting after this guy in the helicopter who messed up our supply line—or, I mean, our supply chain?"

"Well, maybe soon. But not today." El Raton smiled, again. He was in a peaceful mood.

*   *   *

While Francel Williams was in his office questioning the tool pusher, Robert Herrick was in his own office, taking the deposition of Emerald's Vice President of Production. The same VP who had ordered replacing the drilling mud.

"And what did Mr. Dunkelman say to you about your plan to replace the drilling mud with sea water?"

"Nothing in particular that I recall," was the man's answer.

"Did he tell you anything to the effect that he disagreed about replacing the mud?"

The VP smiled. "Not really."

"Why do you say 'not really' instead of No?"

"We discussed all about it, the advantages and disadvantages, just the way we would about any decision on the platform."

Another smile. Robert silently marveled at the way some people can smile while they lie.

"What disadvantages?"

"It might slow us down, having less mud. It might mean we'd have to shut the well in. But both of us thought that was unlikely. So we decided to do what we did."

"Mr. Dunkelman didn't say anything to you about the fact it might not be safe to replace drilling mud with sea water?"

The VP bristled, and he wobbled a little, but he kept his smile. "Not at all. I think you'll find that no one suspected that this might happen."

"What caused it then, according to you?"

"It was an Act of God. And an unavoidable accident."

After that, Robert had to work hard at concentrating, because the contradiction was blatant. There was a huge difference between what the VP was saying and what he knew Dunkelman was saying to Francel Williams right now, across town. He worked hard at staying focused. A few hours later, he felt that he had gotten all of this VP's story. Such as it was.

"That's all," he said finally.

18

The passage of time can be good for negotiations. A meeting that dissolves without any progress can be resumed with everyone on the same page, weeks or months later.

That was what Pepper's lawyer hoped for now, as he met for the second time with the assistant DA who was handling the driving-while-intoxicated case against Pepper. The nineteenth floor of the Criminal Courts Building had neat, spare courtrooms with light carpets, light walls, and dark furnishings. The two lawyers stood, once again, in front of the unoccupied Judge's bench.

"I'm trying to meet you in the middle," said the prosecutor. "No, I can't do probation on an intoxication assault case, and we both know that."

"Well, it's not a real intoxication assault case, and we both know that, too." Pepper's lawyer smiled and adopted a pleasant voice. He was trying to keep it positive. "So, if not probation, what can you do?"

"I'll meet you halfway. A second driving while intoxicated case might get thirty days in jail. The first DWI isn't in the indictment, since it's indicted as an intoxication assault, so it's technically not a second DWI. I'll reduce it to driving while intoxicated and agree to fifteen days instead."

"I don't think . . . I can do that."

"What's your counteroffer? Make it close to fifteen, at least."

"I was thinking, seven. Meet me halfway one more time. Seven days in the County Jail. Which would seem like an eternity to anyone serving it. And please, let us have weekend service of the sentence, because she has a job. If you'll go for that, I'll recommend it to her."

The state's file for the case was sitting on the counsel table, and the assistant DA stared at the cover for a moment. Here, every prosecutor wanted to dispose of misdemeanor cases quickly so that they didn't burden the docket and interfere with handling serious felonies. Then, still hesitating, he said, "O-o-o-kay. I can . . . do that."

The defense lawyer hustled over to Pepper, who sat beside her husband Jonathan. He had discussed the possibility of a lot more than seven days with her. "Good news," he told her. "The DA says three and a half weekends. Seven days, and you can stay free during the week. You'll only have to go to jail three and a half times, and only on the weekends."

Pepper brightened. She had expected it to be a lot worse. Her lawyer had told her that he feared it would be a heavier sentence, because the evidence of her intoxication was overwhelming. There had been an accident, and a man was injured. And she had a prior conviction. "Yes. I'll take that deal," she sighed.

Pepper had followed her lawyer's advice, and she looked like a preppy at an expensive day school getting ready to go to the chapel. She wore a navy suit and a white blouse with lace at the top. Her blonde hair was short. She had used makeup, but minimally and carefully. She seemed taller than her five-foot-six-inch height because she wore three-inch navy heels in a conservative style.

A few minutes later, she was participating with the assistant DA and the judge in the short but formal ceremony that accompanies a plea of guilty.

* * *

Meanwhile, a few blocks to the west, Robert Herrick stood just outside the heavy main doors of the Chase Tower, at the top of the granite steps. He faced a battery of press cameras.

Mr. Herrick," a reporter asked, "why do you think Emerald's man on the platform contradicted their Vice President? It sounds like strange testimony."

Robert asked himself, Why have the inconsistencies in these depositions created so much media interest? There had been bigger events during the Emerald Rose Case that the press hadn't covered.

But there was no accounting for the news cycle. Maybe the other breaking stories were too boring in comparison to a discrepancy that showed that someone was lying. And maybe it was a bigger deal than just a lie, since it was a lie about twenty-seven deaths.

Finally, he had received so many calls for on-camera interviews that he had solved the problem by announcing this press conference.

"Why the contradiction?" Robert shook his head before he answered the question. "Obviously, someone isn't telling the truth."

"Is this the biggest offshore disaster in history?" another reported wanted to know.

"No. The greatest loss of life, ever, was the Piper Alpha Disaster. That was a blowout and explosion in the North Sea near Scotland. It killed more than a hundred people."

"But there also were more than a hundred workers on the Emerald Rose. Why was it that the death toll got held down, here?"

"We were lucky, if you want to call it that, to have only twenty-seven deaths. One difference was the living quarters. The Federal Government reacted to the Piper Alpha Disaster by requiring habitations on offshore rigs to be blast resistant. It wasn't because of any safety concern by Emerald Petroleum, that's for sure."

The next question reminded Robert of the danger of press conferences. During ongoing litigation, an interview with the press is a minefield.

"Back to the contradiction between the stories of the tool pusher and the VP. Which one is it, who's wrong? Who is it, who isn't telling the truth?"

At this stage in the litigation, he told himself, you can't tell what's going to happen. You don't know here the truth is finally going to be found. He remembered a longtime trial lawyer telling him, during his first year, "In a lawsuit, there is no such thing as 'the facts.' There are only pieces of evidence, like tiny parts of a jigsaw puzzle. They can mislead you. They also can be flat-out false. And you can ruin your case with bad guesses."

He dodged the question. "Well, I don't want to be trying this case in the newspapers. Even though I sure do like all of you news guys." He smiled. "We'll have to try the case in the courtroom."

Then, he waved his hand. "I really can't say any more. And I'd better get back to representing my clients."

The reporters shouted more questions. They followed him as he walked toward the door and into the building.

* * *

El Raton paced back and forth in the great room of his home, waving his arms. The big windows let in a magnificent view of the mountains, in rows and undulating rows, but El Raton didn't notice.

"Another shipment lost! The Coast Guard boarded our supposedly safe vessel and stole all of our goods last night. It's our property, and these Gringo bandits just took it!"

"Not only that," said Charro, his first lieutenant. "There's also a whole crew arrested, and we can't ignore the possibility that they're talking to the United States DOJ. The Department of Justice."

"I know." El Raton's voice rose. "I don't care personally about those morons on that boat, of course. They're losers, who gave away our shipment. I don't care if they spend fifteen years in jail. Meanwhile, the danger is small that it will cause any reaction in Mexico that could touch us here in the mountains."

El Raton was wound up, now. "But these days, there's more and more of this kind of thing. And every time, it risks a government invasion of our territory, this place that is mine."

"Not likely."

"Be careful, Charro. What was once improbable, or even impossible, is much more likely today. The central government, together with the army and a lot of uninformed Mexican people—well, they're all united against us. I don't understand it, of course, because we are patriots. We are the entrepreneurs who make this country great."

"That's the truth. We could get away without paying taxes, here in the mountains. But you, Jefe, always work with the Tamaulipas *gobierno*. You negotiate a fair amount that we pay, every year, for the good of all of Tamaulipas."

El Raton brightened a little. "Absolutely. We are good citizens. Good businessmen. And beyond that, we donate to the poor, to the schools, to the church. I guess the people aren't aware of the good deeds that we do."

"We need to advertise, I guess." Charro hoped that his boss would recognize his flair for business.

"Exactly. We need to take action against the cucarachas who've interfered with our supply chain. That would be a helpful kind of advertising."

"Our supply chain is what we live by." Charro understood by now what that meant. "We should take action. You are thinking of that guy who hired the helicopter and spied on us."

"The guy who lives in the Chase Tower. Exactly."

"Exactly, Jefe."

*   *   *

Maria Melendes sat by herself near the mirrored wall in the world-famous restaurant on Bourbon Street. Galatoire's was one of the most elegant places in the Old Quarter of New Orleans. It was known for dishes featuring shrimp, oysters, and trout, but Pompano Pontchartrain was probably its grandest achievement.

Early tomorrow morning, Maria would appear before the Court of Appeals. To represent the State, in the case of Homer Harding. The convict who, while under arrest for murder, had murdered a police officer.

But after a lot of hard work, and feeling tired, she had decided it was time for an excellent dinner.

"Thank you, Richard," she said, as the pompano approached. She always tried to remember the waiters' names here at Galatoire's, because they all had years of service at this desirable job. They were the soul of New Orleans, and they were smart and fun to talk to.

She sat still while the elegantly tuxedoed waiter carefully placed the pompano next to her, almost floating in its Pontchartrain sauce. Then, she lifted her glass of Macon Blanc. "Here's to seeing you again, Richard, and here's to many more visits in the future."

The waiter smiled broadly, showing a gold-covered tooth. He spoke with the prototypical New Orleans accent. "And that's a big back-at-ya', Mademoiselle Maria. You come back any time, and I'll be heah for you."

"But not during Mardi Gras."

"No, not Mardi Gras, or even right befoah. I try to stay away myself. Every fraternity kid from eight states around lands heah on Bourbon Street during Mardi Gras. They party, they block even the sidewalk, they drink like SpongeBob Squarepants. And they get theyah silly selves arrested."

"Well, I'm with you. One time during Mardi Gras is enough. In fact, it's more than enough, I'd say."

"Well, this heah is a better time. Exactly tonight. Music comin in a minute."

"Oh, really?

Richard left to get back to work, and Maria took out her notes. As a veteran of many arguments in courts of appeals, she had a simple method. Everything was handwritten on one manila folder. Written directly on the cream-colored cardstock itself. The inside right page outlined her main argument. The inside left spelled out several points that she would argue if need be. If the questions came up. The back was filled with case authorities, if those came up.

This way, she could open one piece of paper on the podium. Without fumbling. A minor point, but possibly important. She avoided the delay and discomfort that came from having to hunt for her notes in a wad of paper. And this way, she projected to the judges a smooth kind of competence.

She looked at the right inside page. "Actual Innocence of the Death Penalty," she had written. "Applies to new evidence showing subject guilty of murder, but not subject to D Penalty. But doesn't apply here. Claim's not new. Was developed at trial and rejected."

At that moment, a musician stepped into the room carrying a big bass fiddle. Then a banjo player. And last, a man with a saxophone.

Maria thought about the last time she had come to New Orleans for an argument. She had announced to the court that the State would not pursue the death penalty. The Governor, that very morning, had commuted the petitioner's sentence to life without parole.

Some cases end that way.

The judges, or at least one of them, had treated her like a criminal herself. Unfortunately, this Court of Appeals was not what it had been in better times.

But she was confident that tomorrow's argument would go better. Not that she was confident of the court's deciding in her favor. That was too unpredictable to call in any major criminal appeal. But her argument here was solid.

The first musician planted his stand-up bass next to a table and fingered the strings. The saxophone started to moan. The banjo player strummed and sang the first lines of *Basin Street Blues*, with a heavy New Orleans accent that was artificial but effective. "Basin Street . . .

dat's de street ... Wheah all them char-ack-tuhs from the foist precinct meet. . . ."

It was all too good to ignore. Maria set her manila folder aside and paid attention to her Pompano Pontchartrain. And also, she took in the old-time Dixieland that now filled the room.

19

Jimmy Coleman stared at the expert witness. This was his seventeenth deposition this month, but he showed no sign of tiring. His eyes were a colorless gray and his nose was bulbous and red. The man he was questioning looked at Jimmy, and involuntarily, he turned away.

"Doctor Schuster," Jimmy was saying, "what are all of the reasons you now claim that anyone was careless or at fault, in causing the incident on the Deepwater Rose?"

The depositions of the expert witnesses had begun. There still were plaintiffs—family members—whom Jimmy wanted to question, but those would be scheduled when it was possible.

Jimmy started every expert deposition with the same words. For example, he always asked what the witness "now claimed." The word "claim" was designed to suggest something like, "We know you're gonna be lying, you faker, but let's hear what you 'claim.'" The word "now" was there to convey the impression that the witness had told the truth at some time in the past, but "now," he was likely to testify to a doctored-up story.

The witness happened to be a petroleum engineer who'd been engaged by the plaintiffs to provide an opinion about the way the accident had happened. He was a veteran of courtroom conflict and was unfazed, so far, by Jimmy's insinuations.

"There were so many things that were done wrong that it's hard to keep them all straight," he said. "I'll tell you the reasons that occur to me now, about why this disaster happened. First thing, Emerald ignored the fact that gas was bubbling into the formation and through

94

the drilling mud. In fact, it had entered the drill stem. And that's a warning that a blowout may be imminent."

"Anything else?" Jimmy's voice was like a revved-up outboard motor.

"Surely. The casing wasn't rated highly enough. It wasn't substantial enough. An insufficient casing, and you end up with the pressure wandering through leaks."

"Anything else?"

"Again, yes. The decision to proceed with injecting too much sea water in place of mud was just plain dangerous."

"Anything else?"

"That's what I recall now. It just was a whole series of actions."

"Mr. Witness, I'm entitled to know all of your allegations against Emerald Petroleum, not just some of them. All of them. If that's all, can you please tell us that's all?"

Addressing the man as "Mr. Witness" was impersonal and slightly demeaning, and Jimmy intended the insult. But Robert held himself back, because it wasn't against the rules.

"That's all that I recall." The witness was tough. "And I might add that we've been getting information from Emerald in drips and drabs. The Federal Bureau of Mines and Minerals is doing its own investigation, of course, and it's been stonewalled too by your client."

"For the record, I object to the nonresponsive answer."

Robert Herrick was sitting next to his expert witness. This was very satisfying testimony. So far, at least.

But the next thing that happened was that Jimmy looked up sharply, as though he had suddenly discovered something important. Robert was sure it was only an act, but it seemed to have an effect on the witness. "Mr. Witness, you haven't mentioned the Blowout Preventer as something that went wrong. It was installed and handled by Dalliman Services."

"But . . . . You asked me about Emerald Petroleum."

Jimmy turned toward the head of the table. "Ms. Court Reporter, please read back the question that was asked about five questions back. The question that contained the word, 'anyone.'"

The court reporter fumbled with a stack of paper-feed. Finally, she read it. *"Doctor Schuster, what are all of the reasons you now claim* that anyone was careless or at fault, in causing the incident we're talking about?"

She looked at the paper. "Anyone. Yes, it does say, 'anyone.'"

Jimmy turned to the witness. "The question covered everyone, didn't it? And it wasn't just about Emerald Petroleum, right?"

"I stand corrected." The witness looked down.

"You're supposed to tell the whole truth. But you didn't, did you?"

"I'd have to say, that's right, I didn't."

Robert's feeling of success vanished. At trial, Jimmy could read this question and answer out of context, as part of a campaign to destroy his expert witness. "That guy didn't tell the whole truth, and after some prodding, he had to admit it."

And Jimmy had built up a head of steam, by now. "If the Blowout Preventer had done its job, the blowout wouldn't have happened, right?"

"Well . . . that's right." The witness sounded disoriented.

"So, Mr. Witness, the actions of Emerald Petroleum weren't really the immediate cause of this accident. Isn't that right?" Jimmy's voice sounded like a pile driver that needed a quart of oil.

"I guess you could say that."

The deposition went on for three more hours. Three hours, during which the witness rocked and reeled.

At the end, Robert could only say, we haven't officially lost. . . . Yet.

But Jimmy had made today into a very bad day.

* * *

The Court of Appeals Building in New Orleans looks "federal." Anyone who saw it would say, "Hey! That's got to be a federal building." It looks like a big gray mausoleum.

For most criminal cases, this is the final stop. A few cases make it to the Supreme Court, but those are rare, like lottery winners. This place is usually the court of last resort.

Maria Melendes was here to represent the State in the case of Homer Harding. To represent the prosecution. She sat in the audience part of the courtroom, waiting.

Suddenly there were three loud bangs on the back door, which has a big knocker on it for exactly this purpose. A law clerk stepped out to say the traditional words, beginning with "Order in the court. Everyone rise, please. . . ." and ending with, "God save the United States and this Honorable Court."

Three black-robed judges walked in silence to their seats behind the bench. "Be seated, please," said the presiding judge.

He launched into the usual announcements. Every lawyer's speaking time would be strictly measured. The court was familiar with the briefs and knew the facts.

Then, he announced, "The State versus Homer Harding. Habeas corpus petition against a sentence of death." This was Maria's case, the first one on the docket.

"Mr. Santobello," said the judge. This was the name of the lawyer appointed to represent Homer Harding.

The condemned man was not present, of course. There was nothing that he could possibly add, because his word did not matter in this court, on anything. The only issue was whether the trial had somehow been conducted in violation of the Federal Constitution or laws. In fact, anyone who saw one of these habeas corpus arguments for the first time was likely to be struck by how bloodless and boring the entire exercise was. And how little it had to do with murder, or with any crime.

The defense lawyer stepped to the podium. He was tall and slender and wore the lawyer's uniform: a dark pinstriped suit and a red tie. "May it please the Court." This was the traditional opening line.

"Mr. Santobello," said the presiding judge. Which obviously was unnecessary because the Court had just called his name, but this too was traditional.

"Your honors, the second argument in our brief is compelling, I think. The testing of the pistol retrieved from Mr. Harding violated the Fourth Amendment. It was an illegal search and seizure. And all evidence from that testing should have been suppressed and excluded from the trial."

The defense lawyer held up a hand to signal that the next point was important. "There was plenty of time to obtain a warrant. The local police department should have done exactly that—obtained a warrant. Instead, what they did was to perform a trigger-pull test with no preliminaries, with no court authorization, and without the consent of Mr. Harding."

It was a novel argument, at the very least. The judges listened to the lawyer with renewed interest. "In this way, this case resembles *United States v. Jones*," Mr. Santobello went on. "There, the Government attached a GPS locator on the defendant's car and obtained evidence of his travels, which was used to convict him. The Supreme Court said that the search was illegal. The Government should have obtained a warrant."

The presiding judge spoke. "But *Jones* was a case about an electronic device attached to a car. This seizure was of a gun. A pistol. One that everyone knew was used in a crime. Should the police have let Homer Harding keep it?"

"No, your honors." The defense lawyer had anticipated this question. "They had the pistol, properly seized. The public safety exception to the warrant requirement justifies the seizure here, and they had a right to keep the gun safe."

Again, he held up his hand. "But it's the *next* step by the police that violated the law. They attached the gun to a trigger-pull-measurement device. And they pulled the trigger enough to fire the gun. All without a warrant, and without Mr. Harding's consent to this misuse of his property."

The lawyer's voice rose. "And the trigger-pull-device was perfectly analogous to the electronic device in *Jones*. In fact, this measurement used electronic components too. And then, at the trial, the prosecution told the jury how hard the trigger had to be pulled to discharge the gun. They wanted to show that the shot couldn't have been fired by accident, the way the defense claimed. It was crucial evidence."

The judges launched a blizzard of questions about the analogy to the *Jones* case. About the degree of intrusion into the accused's privacy in both cases, the time length, and the way in which the Government's installation of the device in *Jones* was done, in secret.

It wasn't until after that, that the defense lawyer brought up the argument that Maria had thought was the primary issue. The so-called "actual innocence" claim.

Finally, a red light showed on the podium. "I see that my time is up. Thank you, your honors."

"Thank you, Mr. Santobello."

20

What did we do wrong with that expert deposition?" Robert Herrick asked. "I mean, Doctor Schuster just collapsed."

"I don't know," Tom Kennedy replied. "We certainly prepared Dr. Schuster to be questioned as an expert witness. We predicted most of the lines of attack Jimmy Coleman used. We told Dr. Schuster in detail what Jimmy's strategy would be, including trying to get him flustered. We did a practice run, with me asking him Jimmy-Coleman-like questions. But Jimmy flustered him anyway."

"And Tom, when you played the role of Jimmy, I thought you were pretty good at being a jerk."

"Hah, hah."

They sat, as usual, in Robert's office, by the floor-to-ceiling windows. Outside, a wet mist covered the glass with droplets of moisture. The greensward around Buffalo Bayou was visible and shiny with water, but the fog covered the park and horizon in the distance.

"So, then, what did we do wrong?" Robert asked again.

"Robert, you can't always be thinking you did something wrong whenever there's bad luck. If we did anything wrong, it was to get Dr. Schuster as an expert witness. But that actually wasn't something we did wrong, either. The guy has solid gold credentials and even a track record of testifying as an expert."

"I guess so. What I'm trying to do is to learn something from this experience."

"Sometimes you can learn something from a bad experience. But it's just as important not to learn something that isn't there."

At that, Robert laughed. But there was a twitch of pain in his laugh.

"Besides," Tom said, "it isn't the end of the world. As usual, Jimmy showed that he's a total sleazebag. If he plays very much of the deposition on the monitor in front of the jury, he's going to lose more than he can possibly gain."

"He doesn't have to play very much to make his point. He might only play the question and answer about Dr. Schuster admitting that he didn't tell the 'whole truth.'"

"If that's all he shows the jury, it's not going to make much of an impression. Besides, you can clear it up with Dr. Schuster on the stand. You'll say, 'What did you mean?' And he'll say, 'Only that I left something out.' And then we can play the whole sequence of questions leading up to that and show Jimmy for what he is."

Robert smiled. "Okay, Tom. You've got me pegged. I'm an overachiever and something of a pessimist."

Tom laughed again. "Every trial lawyer is like that, if they're any good at all."

* * *

Back in New Orleans, Maria Melendes was still at the Court of Appeals. The defense lawyer had just argued on behalf of Homer Harding. He had made his case for the man who, while under arrest for murder, had murdered the police officer who was driving him to jail.

Now it was Maria's job to respond, on behalf of the prosecution.

She walked quickly to the podium. "May it please the Court."

"Ms. Melendes."

"The petitioner argues that the testing of the gun used to kill the police officer was an illegal search and seizure. We disagree.

"Mr. Santobello seems to concede that there was probable cause for the trigger-pull test. He has to, because of course there was probable cause. And although he is very competent, Mr. Santobello has found no cases that back his extraordinary argument. Absolutely no cases to support him. Trigger-pull tests have been performed without warrants since time immemorial, and if there were a credible argument that all of them were illegal searches, you would expect there to be cases saying so. But there are none."

She gestured slightly. "Also, the *Jones* case isn't analogous to this case, at all. Here, the police possessed the gun, and they possessed it properly. Everybody agrees to that. In *Jones,* the defendant possessed the car that was being followed by the GPS device, and he continued to possess it after the device was attached. In fact, that was the point. In *Jones,* the device was planted to record where the defendant drove the car.

"Besides, in this case, once the officers seized the pistol—and they did it lawfully—they did nothing further that interfered with the defendant's privacy or possession of the gun. The trigger test simply had nothing to do with anything the Fourth Amendment is designed to protect."

Her adrenalin was flowing. "So, this wasn't an illegal search. First, there are no cases, when there would be, if the petitioner were correct; second, the police were the ones who rightfully possessed the gun, not the defendant; and third, there was no interference with any interest that the Fourth Amendment protects."

Next, there was the usual barrage of questions from the judges. And after that, Maria answered the other arguments that Homer Harding's lawyer had raised, one by one.

Too soon, the red light flashed to signal the end. There wasn't enough time for all she had to say, because there never was. She sat down and packed up while the lawyers in the next case crept up to the counsel tables. Outside, she smiled and shook hands with Harding's lawyer, Santobello. He had done a capable but ethical job for the client he had been appointed to represent.

And she hailed a taxi to travel to the airport, and from there, back home. Tomorrow she would wear her biggest dark glasses and most nondescript jacket, because she expected to have to shove her way to the courthouse through a whole tribe of "Free Homer" protesters.

Some time in the future, which could be two weeks or two years away, the Court of Appeals would write an opinion either affirming or reversing the judgment against Homer Harding.

* * *

Meanwhile, back in his office, Robert Herrick was explaining a new event to his client. "This is a messy development," he said.

Randy Westhoven and Tom Kennedy sat in front of Robert's desk. Randy looked for an instant out the big windows toward the horizon.

Randy looked puzzled. "As the non-lawyer here, I have to admit, I don't understand what it's about."

"That's okay. And it's not surprising. But I want you to understand what's going on. Jimmy Coleman has filed what's called a 'Motion for Summary Judgment' against us. To repeat, it's called a *Motion for Summary Judgment,* and let me explain."

"A Motion for what?"

"A Motion for Summary Judgment. Here's what that's about. Jimmy is saying that the case is so clear that a trial is not needed. He wins right now. Or so he claims. The case can be handled in a 'summary' manner, meaning without a trial. Because it's so clear, he says."

"If the case is so clear, what's clear is that our side wins, not the defendants. Jimmy Coleman is just plain wrong."

Robert smiled. "We think so too. But I want you to understand Jimmy's argument. I'll need to communicate with all of the plaintiffs, and talking it over with you, Randy, will help me to explain it to everyone else."

"All right. Yes, tell me about it."

"Here's Jimmy's basic argument. Our expert petroleum engineer has testified that if the Blowout Preventer had worked, this disaster wouldn't have happened. That's true, of course. And the Blowout Preventer was Dalliman's responsibility, not Emerald Petroleum's. So mishandling the Blowout Preventer isn't the fault of Jimmy's client. Or so he says."

"So far, I follow you."

"And from that, Jimmy argues that his client, Emerald, did not cause this event. Dalliman did."

"Well, I suppose that's true, in a way. But so what?"

"Jimmy's argument, on Emerald Petroleum's behalf, is that we— the plaintiffs—have to prove that his client, Emerald Petroleum caused the accident. But he says that since Dalliman actually was the one that caused it, according to him, we can't prove that Emerald caused it. And our expert witness does, indeed, say that the Blowout Preventer could have prevented it."

"And that's Emerald Petroleum's argument, concocted by Jimmy Coleman?"

"Yes. It's a simplified version of the argument, because Jimmy has a lot of rhetorical flourishes, and he cites a lot of cases, but that's the guts of it."

"Well, why . . . . Why did we hire an expert who said it was Dalliman's fault?"

"Well, because that's the truth. Yes, it was Dalliman's fault. But Jimmy's trying to take that one giant leap farther. He's trying to say that since it was Dalliman's fault, it couldn't also be Emerald Petroleum's fault. In his mind, Dalliman's negligence cancels out Emerald's negligence."

"That can't be the law."

"Right. It certainly isn't. And we will vigorously oppose this Motion for Summary Judgment. But as I was saying, it makes things messy. We'll have to divert a lot of our effort into our opposition to this motion that Jimmy has filed, even though we think it's dead wrong. That's probably what Jimmy intends. To sidetrack us and make us waste a lot of time. And, of course, there's one more problem with it."

"What's that?"

"No matter how hard we fight against this, there's always a slim chance that the judge might actually buy the argument. There's always that tiny chance. We'll have to work hard and be sure we get the judge to understand what's going on. And Jimmy's counting on our having to do a lot of work. A lot of useless effort. It didn't take much for him to file this motion, and he's using it to divert our efforts from preparing the case for trial."

Robert smiled, to avoid showing his concern. "We can't afford to let that tiny chance happen, of course."

21

The intercom buzzed. "Robert, it's your favorite detectives," Donna deCarlo told him. "Derrigan Slaughter and Donnie Cashdollar. Both of them are on the line. They say it's important."

"Okay." He was puzzled, because he wasn't expecting anything involving the police.

"And they say they'll need to talk to Tom Kennedy, too," Donna added. "It's some kind of problem involving Tom. I've already buzzed him and told him to come to your office."

"Thanks. You're always efficient. Put them through."

"Hello, gentlemen." Robert grinned, because these two detectives were good friends, by now. "I've got the speaker on so Tom can hear. What's up?"

Tom Kennedy walked in, sat down, and said, "Hello, detectives. You're my favorite cops, and it's always nice to hear from you. But I guess I should wait to hear what you have to tell us, before I say that."

"Right. It ain't nothin pretty."

Robert thought about the first time he had met these two detectives, in a case years ago. Derrigan Slaughter was an elegantly dressed black man who had worn a perfectly fitted navy suit and a solid red tie. Donnie Cashdollar, on the other hand, had sported a disconnected smorgasbord of colors and styles: a green shirt, brown jacket, blue tie, and gray slacks. The dress code these two officers followed was familiar to Robert by now, and in fact the people at the police department had stopped making jokes about it because it was so familiar.

Robert thought to himself, once again, about the names of these two partners. Slaughter, he had concluded, was a perfect name for a homicide detective. But Cashdollar didn't fit. That guy ought to transfer, maybe to the forgery division. But he didn't say anything out loud about it. He just contented himself, now, with a tiny smile.

"We got some a' this here gang intelligence," Detective Slaughter announced. "It's got yo' name on it, Tom."

Donnie Cashdollar spoke up. "We can't tell exactly what's going on. But Tom, it's possible out there, that there may be a hit on you, contracted out."

"What?" Tom was dumfounded.

"It be a . . . contract murder that's been planned, we think." Slaughter's voice was hesitant. "But I gotta say it again. We ain't exactly sure. That's the way this here gang intelligence comes to us."

"Why me?"

"That's something once more that we don't know fo' sure. Best we can tell, it's somebody in Mexico connected with drug smuggling."

"Which is very bad news," said Cashdollar, stating the obvious. "And which, we can guess, maybe has something to do with these outlaws thinking that you've messed with their business, or that you might be gonna interfere somehow."

"I don't know of anything like that."

"Well, think over the last few months, which is when we think it came up. It may not be anything you really did. But if this information is real, they must think you did something. Or that you might do something."

Robert was amazed too. "Tom, I can't imagine. . . ."

"I can't imagine anything either."

Silence. It persisted for more than a moment.

"You know, Tom," Robert said finally. "Remember, in the helicopter, what we saw out by the Emerald Rose platform."

"Ahhhh. . . ." Tom was still trying to absorb it.

"We hired a helicopter. Actually, Tom hired it, and I guess his name surfaced that way. And we went to investigate one of our cases. And we saw a guy on this burned-out oil well—you know, the Emerald Rose well—attaching something to the platform. And there was another ship coming to pick it up. The helicopter pilot radioed the Coast

Guard, and a big cutter was in the area. The Coast Guard must have shut down the smugglers and seized a big package of drugs."

"That fits, from what we done heard." Detective Slaughter sounded sympathetic.

The light was dawning on Tom. "I . . . I need some kind of protection."

"The bad news is, we can't give you none by the po-lice, at least not on a continuous basis. It takes a huge number of officers to provide consistent protection. Two for each a' three shifts, and a bunch more for days and nights when those guys ain't on the job. Takes too many po-licemen away from what they usually be doin. Police protection, that's in the movies."

Tom was very, very quiet.

"Well, you know," Robert said, "we've got an extra room here in the office, with a complete setup for a guest. I use it sometimes when I pull an all-nighter. And of course we've got twenty-four hour security, because of what's happened to us in the past."

Tom was still quiet.

"Tom," Robert said, "Pack your bag. Stay here until the whole thing passes."

"That'd be a good idea," Slaughter agreed.

* * *

"Damn," said Wendy Bachman, the cussing Mormon.

"It's terrible." Maria sat down next to Wendy's desk, in front of the appellate section at the DA's office. "Why has the Court of Appeals decided in favor of Homer Harding, of all people?"

"These Court of Appeals judges have decided to turn this murdering fucker, this Homer Harding, loose?" Wendy was amazed. "Don't they know that he was under arrest for murder at the time he murdered this police officer?"

"Of course they do. But that doesn't have anything to do with the case."

"Things would be a damn sight better if I ran the Supreme Court."

"You'd give 'em some four letter words, wouldn't you? But in these kinds of cases, the horror of the crime doesn't usually matter. It's about whether the defendant's rights were violated. The defendant's federal rights."

"Like this search-and-seizure BS about the trigger-pull test."

"Well, yes. The trouble is, the way the judges see it, the search-and-seizure stuff isn't BS. They think the defense argument is righteous."

"They think this rat bastard's right to privacy was violated? I guess he is a very delicate sort of guy who has an exaggerated sense of his important self, even though he's a multiple murderer."

Maria didn't answer. She sat down to reread the Court of Appeals opinion, which sent Homer Harding's petition for habeas corpus back down to the federal district judge with directions to grant it. If that happened, Homer Harding would get a new trial in state court. With the evidence of the trigger-pull test excluded. And that trigger-pull test was strong evidence against the defense theory that the gun just sort of discharged accidently.

And now, the jury wouldn't hear about the trigger-pull test at all.

The Court's opinion was long. About twenty pages. Sometimes length is an indicator of a dubious conclusion, especially with a meandering explanation like this one. The Court of Appeals had written at length about how the Founding Fathers had created the Bill of Rights with exactly this kind of "trespass upon privacy" in mind. The English Government had used so-called "writs of assistance" to authorize searches that broke into multiple people's homes without probable cause. And that, the judges said, was what the Fourth Amendment was all about. Preventing the trespasses that the British had committed.

Maria saw that the judges had accepted completely the defense lawyer's argument about the case of *United States v. Jones*. So, the Supreme Court said in the *Jones* case that attaching a GPS monitor to the bottom of a car, without a warrant, was an illegal search? Well, the Court of Appeals said, "a trigger-pull test is just like a GPS monitor. It uses electronics, too."

"There is no difference," the judges said, "between using a GPS device to record the pathway of a vehicle and using a trigger-pull device to measure tension in a gun."

And the fact that the police had the right of possession of the gun was irrelevant. The defendant still owned the gun. The judges said that privacy was a "precious jewel." And "Homer Harding's precious right of privacy in his pistol requires protection here, just as the defendant's car did in *United States v. Jones*."

Maria wondered what to do next. Should the prosecution file a petition with the Supreme Court, trying to get the Court of Appeals opinion reversed? That might take years. And from what she recalled, the Supreme Court gets more than seven thousand petitions a year, and it agrees to hear only a few more than a hundred. The odds were not good.

Maybe the District Attorney's office should just retry Homer Harding, the way that the Court of Appeals had ordered. The defensive theory about the gun going off accidently was absurd, even without trigger-pull evidence. But that, of course, would mean that all of the loops of appeals and habeas corpus petitions would start all over again from the beginning, not to mention the trial itself. And that process would take even more years.

Maria shook off her disappointment and started writing a memorandum to the District Attorney about what to do next.

22

Judge Pamela Preston ascended to the bench. Her courtroom, like all federal courtrooms, was built to display the power and dignity of the Government. The bench sat high above the floor, wide and dark, and it was backed by a granite facing that stood twenty feet over the judge, dramatically setting her off against the wooden paneling.

"I have four complex hearings to finish in a really short time," the judge announced. "It is now ... nine in the morning. I have a jury appearing at ten, so I have one hour. First case is Wooten Electrical Inc. versus The Harishoner Company."

She pointed downward. "Lawyers, get to the point quickly."

The first case was a dispute about discovery that the defendant wanted to get from the plaintiff. It would require thousands of particularized, hard-to-find documents. Judge Preston heard arguments for less than ten minutes before saying, "The motion is granted. Defendant, prepare me an order."

She looked at the docket. "Next, it's Westhoven versus Emerald Rose Petroleum Company. Defendant Emerald, you have a Motion for Summary Judgment."

An army of lawyers came forward. Jimmy Coleman sat on one side of the courtroom. Ironically, the other three defendants—Dalliman, Momex, and Amadanko—were on the same side as Westhoven, the plaintiff. They opposed Jimmy's motion, because if he were to be successful in getting Emerald Petroleum out of the case, the other three would be responsible for the entire judgment.

"Mr. Coleman?"

"It's simple, your honor. Our brief is short, and it says it all, because this case is clear. The Blowout Preventer was not Emerald's responsibility at all. It was manufactured, installed, maintained, and operated by Dalliman Services, alone. The plaintiff's expert testified that if the Blowout Preventer had worked right, there would have been no blowout, and the testimony is quoted in our brief. Emerald Petroleum simply did not cause this accident. And your honor has very few cases that are so straightforward, because that's the whole case."

"Mr. Herrick?"

"Your honor, there can be concurrent causes. Two or more defendants can be negligent at the same time, and they cause an accident together. It happens all the time. The tort law says that there can be more than one proximate cause, and it's such a common principle of law that whenever there's a jury instruction on negligence, the jury is told explicitly that there can be more than one proximate cause. Here, one cause was Dalliman, it's true; but Emerald Petroleum was a concurrent cause. We've cited the cases in our brief."

Now, Jimmy waved his arms. "Concurrent causes can exist, your honor—yes. But that's not what we have here. The Blowout Preventer failure was first. Primary. And completely independent from what Emerald may have done. That device was supposed to ensure that there would be no blowout. It was only after that event that Emerald's actions mattered at all. Mr. Herrick's own expert says so."

He pointed at Dalliman's lawyers. "The chain of causation was broken. We've cited the cases about that in our brief. This is a classic case of a party, namely Emerald, not being the cause, because the chain of causation was broken by an independent cause, namely Dalliman."

The judge shook her head. "I doubt that the precise time sequence of momentary events matters when there's concurrent causation. Was Emerald negligent before the Blowout Preventer failed, if it did? Or was Dalliman first? I don't think it matters. It's going to be up to the jury to decide the proximate cause question. The Motion for Summary Judgment is denied. Mr. Herrick, prepare an order."

But the judge's voice rose. "I have to add, Mr. Herrick, that you will have a big hill to climb during a jury trial, if there is one. The jury will have to decide not only who was negligent, but also who was the proximate cause. Mr. Coleman can make his argument to the jury, the same one he's made here. And Mr. Herrick, you're in danger of losing that fight."

Every judge wants every case to settle. And so Judge Preston shook her head again. "Look, Mr. Herrick, settle this case if you possibly can. Mr. Coleman, you can lose too, so be generous with your own settlement negotiations. Both sides. All sides, including all of the defendants, hear me. Get together—and *settle* this case!"

"Well," Robert said to Tom as they left the courtroom, "I thought we had the better of the argument on the Motion for Summary Judgment. But now, the judge seems to think that Jimmy's going to have a powerful argument in front of the jury.

"And she may make rulings during the trial with that in mind, which will help Jimmy beat us. I wonder whether we really won this hearing."

* * *

Nightfall. Robert knocked. And opened Rosalie Herrick's door. "Hi, Mama. Ahhh. Hi . . . Rosalie."

"My little Robert! What did you play at today?"

Robert laughed. "I played at being a lawyer."

"And did you do stuff like argue with people? And cross-examine them?"

"That's right."

"That's good. Long as you're just playing. But always remember, son, that when it comes down to really accomplishing things, you're always better off getting along."

He looked up sharply. "What do you mean?"

"There's an old saying. *You can catch more bears with honey than with a club.*"

He stared at her. And later, driving home, he thought, "You get advice to use in your lawsuits from the strangest places."

* * *

In this jurisdiction, it is practically impossible to get a trial setting without going through mediation. The judges believe in mediation, and they have the power to make you use it. This process—

mediation—results in the settlement of most of the claims where trial settings would otherwise be asked for.

At precisely nine o'clock in the morning, the court-appointed mediator for the Emerald Rose case sat at the head of a very long table. He was a young lawyer, but he had had plenty of trial experience. His hair was cropped short, and he wore a light blue sports jacket with a blue tie.

The mediator started with the usual speech, explaining what mediation was. "I myself have no power except to persuade. I'm on everybody's side and nobody's side. I'm just an advocate for settlement."

He looked at all four parties. He nodded at Robert Herrick and Randy Westhoven on one side of the table, and the four defendants and their lawyers on the other. "This is a private zone for negotiation. Mediation is nothing more than fancy, assisted negotiation. I'll be helping you and urging you to settle. And so, what I'm saying is different from the so-called *Miranda* warnings that you get when you're arrested. Here, you can say anything while you're trying to settle this case, and it *can never* be used against you."

This mediator seemed decisive and energetic, and Robert had hopes that he would get the case settled at a fair amount. That would be nice.

You can catch more bears with honey that with a club, he told himself. Maybe it will work.

The mediator turned to him. "Mr. Herrick, your opening statement?"

"All four of the defendants were negligent, and all four were concurrent causes of this disaster." Robert said it evenly, but emphatically. "I'll start with Emerald Petroleum. All of you know the acts that our complaint charges against Emerald, and there is no question that they can be proved."

He held up one finger. "First, Emerald used an inadequate casing for the pressure." Next, two fingers. "Emerald ignored the warning devices showing that gas was leaking into the wellhead, which is an unmistakable signal that a blowout is likely." Three fingers. "Emerald substituted sea water for drilling mud that was holding down the pressure, which brought on the blowout in a matter of seconds."

He took his fingers down. "There are other acts of negligence, but that's enough for now. And Emerald pushed everyone to avoid raising safety concerns, because it valued money over human beings."

Next, he plowed through the negligent acts of Dalliman, Momex, and Amidanko. Then, it was time to discuss damages.

"Twenty-seven people dead. Vaporized or lost at sea. Many more badly hurt, with life-changing injuries. Some with life-ruining injuries, in fact. More than a hundred plaintiffs, including spouses and family. All of you defendants are familiar with the damages, actually, because of discovery in this case. Medical records galore, and lots of other sources of information."

He paused. "Our demand for settlement is eight hundred million dollars, and we expect to prove every cent if this case goes to trial."

Then, he remembered. Honey, rather than a club. "We respect every one of you as lawyers. And the defendants, all of you, as competent, diligent companies in the oil patch. We hope that we can work this case out with you."

Robert usually thought that the plaintiff himself ought to say something at a mediation—not anything legalistic, but something about how bad the damages were. How badly he was hurt. Now, he turned to the one representative he had prepared to speak.

"Mr. Westhoven—Randy—can you add anything to that?"

"I'm not a lawyer, of course," the lead plaintiff said. "At times I've been mystified about the legalisms that I've heard in this case. But I don't want you to forget that the deaths and injuries are those of flesh-and-blood people. People like my father."

Randy Westhoven swallowed hard. "My father was my fountain of wisdom when I needed it. He taught me to ride a bicycle when I was four. He taught me to play baseball, and I still play it, as a grownup. And he helped me keep my sanity when my first job ended because the company went bankrupt. I was desperate. I was almost crazy. But my father had the experience to tell me how to handle it."

The lead plaintiff's voice broke. "I miss my father. I love my father. Whenever something important happens, I still think to myself, 'Wait until I tell him about this.'"

He stared at the four defendants. "And then I realize that I can't tell my father anything. And it's because of what your four businesses did. You hurt me. You hurt me very badly."

Perfect, Robert thought. And it sounded unrehearsed.

Even though it had been carefully rehearsed, from beginning to end.

23

The usual approach of a defendant at a mediation is to say, "Mr. Plaintiff, we are genuinely regretful for your loss. However, we do not think we are responsible for it."

But Jimmy Coleman's approach was different.

"Randall Westhoven," he said, "your lawsuit against Emerald Petroleum does not belong in court. Your claims against Emerald are groundless. If we have to defend them in a trial, we are confident of being exonerated. Any jury will pour you right back out of the courthouse and onto the street."

Jimmy sounded like a cement mixer that continued to grind away. "The judge said that if there is a trial, your lawyer will have a hill to climb. She meant that you will face an uphill battle. Your own expert has said that the accident would not have happened if the Blowout Preventer had done its job, and Emerald had no responsibility for the Blowout Preventer."

Jimmy ground on, with mention of the argument that everyone on the platform was a borrowed servant and entitled to recover only worker's compensation insurance. Anyway, he said, the Emerald Rose disaster was an unavoidable accident and an Act of God.

And finally, he got to the point. "We would like to get out of this lawsuit, of course. It is for that reason, and only for that reason, that I am authorized to offer you and all the other plaintiffs a single sum, a total of ten million dollars, for the settlement of all claims. There is a certain nuisance value to any lawsuit. Every lawsuit costs money. The nuisance value of your case is ten million dollars."

Jimmy was followed by lawyers for Dalliman Services, Momex, and Amadanko. Each of them denied liability. They offered to settle for a million dollars each—one tenth of what Emerald wanted to pay.

* * *

The District Attorney's own private office was simple but elegant, as it should be in the nation's third largest city. The District Attorney herself was an elegant woman, well dressed in a St. John knit in a dark red. Her brown hair moved as she shook her head, when Maria Melendes mentioned the decision of the Court of Appeals in the Homer Harding case.

"These are judges with active imaginations. They say that Homer Harding's privacy is a 'precious jewel'? Some law clerk about twenty-three years old must have stayed up all night to write that."

"It's a silly opinion," Maria agreed. "The trouble is, after I went on and on, yelling in my office about how dumb it was and kicking the file cabinet, I realized that we're stuck with it."

"Well, that's true, of course. This office, more than most others, has to keep reminding itself to focus on reality."

"Right. Rather than the how-bad-it-is complaint, we've got to look at the what-to-do-about it question."

"Yes, indeed. And there, the silliness of the opinion will help us. And I notice that it's a two-to-one opinion. One judge dissented."

"Yes. The dissenting judge's opinion came in later. It basically accepted our argument—that the police officers already possessed the gun, and the trigger-pull test was not an interference with any right of privacy of the defendant."

"This is an important case." The District Attorney's voice was thoughtful, now. "It's important to the citizens of this district. They shouldn't have to put up with a murder suspect who commits another murder by shooting and killing an arresting officer. Obviously, it's important to the entire police department."

Maria nodded. "And also, there's the terrible precedent this opinion sets. It will tie police investigations up in knots. We shouldn't let this opinion remain as the last word on this Fourth Amendment question."

"Maria, you've recommended that we try to get the whole Court of Appeals to hear this case. Right now, it's two judges. Two out of three.

There are— how many?—maybe fifteen judges on the Court of Appeals. They can decide to have all of their membership decide the case."

"I'll make a motion to have them do that."

"This pathway will take years to complete, of course."

"That's the way this kind of case goes."

"And if it doesn't work with the Court of Appeals, petition the Supreme Court." The District Attorney smiled. "You've done a good job, Maria, and I know you'll do well at seeing that the silliness of the opinion does matter. It's a bad enough decision to catch the attention of the entire Court of Appeals. Or the highest court we've got."

* * *

Across town, Robert and Jimmy—and the mediator—were still going back and forth for hours with offers and counteroffers. The mediation was sliding into the evening. Six o'clock. Now, seven. The mediator had shuttled a dozen times between the plaintiffs and the defendants—or, sometimes, among defendants, because a major question was, which defendant should pay how much of the damages.

"Latest word from Jimmy Coleman," the mediator announced at seven-thirty. "From Emerald Petroleum. He offers seventy-five million to settle all claims."

"Well, it's a little movement toward a reasonable settlement," Robert answered. "Not even close to what's needed, though."

"Sometimes you have to cut the dog's tail off one inch at a time." The mediator smiled. "Robert, you've been pretty fixed for the last three hours. Your most recent demand only came down from seven hundred million to six hundred seventy-five million. None of the defendants believes you could recover anything like that in a trial."

"I'll agree to recommend six hundred fifty million to my clients."

"Not enough of a reduction. But I'll try with the defendants. By the way, their total, now, is two hundred million, because Dalliman, Momex, and Amadanko's offers add up to a hundred twenty-five million. With Emerald's seventy-five million, that's two hundred. We're getting there."

"Maybe." Robert shook his head. "I don't really have room to go down more, because I can't recommend a lesser amount in good conscience."

"Awww, Robert, you know better than to say that." In spite of his weariness, the mediator chuckled as he walked out to shuttle over to the defendants.

* * *

Nine o'clock. The mediator was still going back and forth among the parties. Shuttle diplomacy. The numbers inched closer together. Later, at midnight, the plaintiff was demanding six hundred million and the defendants were offering three hundred million.

"We'd like to settle this," said the lawyer for Amadanko. "My last offer was thirty million, which I realize is a small part of the six hundred million you're asking for, Robert. But objectively, Amadanko is the least responsible party here."

"Maybe so." Robert was dead tired.

"I'll up it to forty million on behalf of Amadanko. And settle it for Amadanko with you, even if the others don't. Remember, now, I can only agree to recommend it to my client. I have a feeling they'll take it."

"Well, and of course I can only recommend it to my clients too."

"Of course."

"But I'll do that. Forty million. For a hundred clients, after payment of costs and fees, it represents an average amount of two hundred fifty thousand to three hundred thousand dollars each. It's a start toward justice."

"And it's as close to settling the case as you're going to get tonight. Settling with one party, Amadanko. I'll tell you what. I'll tell them to pay it and I won't even look back."

Half an hour later, the mediator gathered everyone but Amadanko together and declared that the negotiations were at an impasse. The mediation was over.

As they walked out, Jimmy still had something to say. And it certainly had the Jimmy Coleman touch.

"Thanks, Herrick, for rejecting our settlement offer, so we can show a jury how piss-poor your case is. How often do we get to try a case that's this big a winner for the defense?"

24

El Raton, standing in his elegant great room, stared out the windows at the bluish-gray mountains of the Sierra Madre.

"Charro, this is going to set us back. Our accounts receivable, I mean."

His voice was angry. It signaled to everyone, even to Charro, that it would be best to remain invisible if you could. When El Raton was angry about matters of finance, that was when he reached his very angriest.

"Yes, Jefe."

Suddenly, El Raton turned around. He faced a paneled wall filled with photographs of himself meeting with the bishop of Tamaulipas and with the governor.

"There are ways that we can get our accounts receivable back to normal, but all of them are risky, and they will take time."

"Yes, Jefe."

El Raton stomped as he turned around again, toward the mountains. "That United States government! It's a criminal organization. Charro, what is the name of the agency in the States that has shut down our corresponding bank?"

"It's called the Federal Deposit Insurance Corporation, Jefe."

"Yes. The FDIC. And what was the reason they shut down our corresponding bank?"

Charro knew it wasn't really a "corresponding bank"—it was really just a way-station on a money laundering trail—but his boss's penchant for business-school terminology led him to call it that.

He was timid about answering. "Jefe, I'm . . . not sure. But I think the FDIC found out about our, ah, commerce with the bank."

"And because we are customers, the FDIC shut down the whole bank?"

"Jefe, I'm . . . not sure."

"That's what I mean. It's a criminal organization, the United States. They find one customer they don't like, and it's unfair in the first place that they don't like us, but on account of that—just that—they shut down the whole blasted bank."

"Jefe, it is unfair. Exactly what you say."

"And us—meanwhile, we get distracted. Our incoming supply chain continues on, and we owe money, and by now we've fixed our outgoing supply chain, but things still don't work, because we can't handle our accounts receivable properly. Because we don't have our corresponding bank. And that distracts us from a lot of other issues."

"Jefe, it sure does. It distracts us."

"For instance, the advertising campaign that you and I talked about a while ago, Charro."

"Advertising, Jefe?" Charro wanted to make a short, sage-sounding noise of agreement, but he didn't recognize El Raton's reference to an advertising campaign.

"Remember that *gusano*—that maggot—the one who flew in with the helicopter and destroyed our supply chain? We worked up all kinds of energy about how he needed to disappear. And that would have been a very nice advertisement, to let everyone know that it isn't smart to insult us. Avertising."

"Oh, yes, Jefe. Yes. Advertising."

"We need to get that done. And we've gotten distracted from it."

* * *

Three hundred and fifty miles to the north, Jimmy Coleman was in the middle of a ritual that he used, every time, to prepare for trial. It was customary.

Trial lawyers are unusual people. And they are unusual among themselves.

Jimmy had spent sixteen hours the day before in conventional kinds of preparation. Figuring out what to say to the jury, how to handle witnesses. That kind of stuff. Now it was time for something different.

At this moment, the head of litigation for Booker and Bayne was sitting in the middle of his living room on an oriental rug, with his legs bent in his best imitation of a yoga position. The bottoms of his flat, chubby feet pointed straight up. He wore a huge silk robe, black with white lapels, the kind a champion boxer might wear while dancing through the crowd toward the ring. But this resplendent, shiny robe was peeled back from his shoulders to show off Jimmy's paunchy stomach, which disappeared into a pair of plaid boxer shorts.

His wife, nearly six feet tall, hovered over him, rubbing scented palm oil into his shoulders. Barbara Coleman had on a black T-shirt with an orange starburst that featured a wicked-looking helicopter above the words, "Soldier of Fortune: The Magazine of Professional Adventurers." Again, this was a customary part of Jimmy's trial preparation. She wore a wide gold choker-type necklace, because this, too, was a fixture of the ritual. She looked like a Viking warrior who'd been transported to the Amazon region, all ready for jungle warfare. Or maybe, a figure from a Wagnerian opera, preparing for the beach.

As Barbara Coleman squeezed the liquid onto Jimmy's splotchy skin, she chanted, "Next week is going to be a great week for Jimmy. Next week is going to a great week for Jimmy."

This was how Jimmy Coleman, for years, had gotten ready to steamroll his opponents. It usually worked, and being a pragmatist, he was careful to preserve even the finer details, down to his wife's customary T-shirt. Jimmy wouldn't have wanted to change any of this strange ceremony, any more than a superstitious baseball player would change his routine before stepping into the batter's box.

He cleared his mind. He kept his eyes shut. And he tried to experience it all: the oil, his Viking wife, and the incantations she repeated. "Next week is going to be a great week for Jimmy. Next week is going to be a great week for Jimmy. . . ."

He stirred. It was time to change the mantra. "Thank you, my love. Now, would you please say it the other way—that it's going to be a bad week for Robert Herrick?"

His model-height wife poured on more palm oil, and then she started the new chant. "Next week is going to be a bad week for Robert Herrick. Next week is going to be a bad week for Herrick. He's going to get broken up into little bitty pieces and flushed right out of court. Next week is going to be a bad week for Herrick."

Jimmy had discovered that for him, it was more useful to trash-talk the other side than it was to build up his own case. He was a street fighter, and he remembered the lessons he had learned there. Picture your opponent as a piece of garbage. As less than human; less than an insect. For Jimmy, it worked. This was an excellent way to prepare for trial, if you were like Jimmy Coleman and you wanted to be successful.

"... A bad week for Herrick. ... Gonna get killed. Slaughtered. Next week is going to be a bad week for Robert Herrick."

Herrick wasn't to be thought of as "learned counsel." And Jimmy wanted to internalize that conviction. Herrick was a slimy, incompetent worm, who shouldn't be a lawyer, much less in the same courtroom with me. Not even as good as an enemy. A slug, a snake, a cockroach. It wasn't necessary to be courteous with him or his clients.

And finally, having achieved that state of mind, Jimmy felt it.

He was ready for trial.

*   *   *

Robert Herrick had worked sixteen hours too. He thought he might be too tired to do anything. Or maybe he was about to catch his second wind.

Here was Maria. She was always the one to get him to put it all in perspective.

"It all starts next week," she said brightly. "Aren't you as ready as you'll ever be?"

"Maybe. But maybe I'm . . . not ready. It's a terrible feeling. I don't want to let my clients down."

"You always think that."

"Maybe. Yes, maybe I always think that."

"You're as ready as you'll ever be."

"Maybe I'm as ready as I'll ever be. But maybe not."

"Well, just so you can be sure, there's another level of trial preparation you can do right now. With me. Right here. Come on." She started unbuttoning her blouse.

"No, Maria. Cut it out. I'm too deep into this trial to think about anything else."

"I did this once before with you, this kind of trial preparation. You said you were tired, but I convinced you. And remember, you won that case big time."

"I remember that occasion. But this case is a completely different. What's gotten into your mind this time?"

"I wouldn't have had the idea, except that I really do think you're as ready as you'll ever be. And also, I like you when you're this tired. Your feeble brain makes you so cute. So, this is the real trial preparation. Come on."

He did what she told him, because he didn't have enough determination to do anything else.

"If you kept worrying, you'd just lose your edge. This is what you need to be doing right now. So, I wonder what part of the trial to take on." She slid her skirt down and shimmied out of it.

"I don't know."

"I do. Maybe the direct examination." Saying that, she dropped her bra and panties onto the floor. "Look here. And this will be followed by the opening and the closing."

"Okay, okay."

"And then, a request for production. And a deposition."

"All right."

"I've said this before, but I don't understand why people think it's fun to play doctor. This is more fun. Playing lawyer."

"Yes, I know. You like playing lawyer. Especially when I'm dead tired."

"Robert, I'm counting on you to win this case." Suddenly, her voice was insistent, heavy, serious. "You didn't even want to take this case. But since you did, you'd better win it."

"That's why I've been doing all this preparation."

"And here's something else I've told you before. If you don't win, I'm going to tell all your associates that the reason you lost was because this was the way you prepared for trial."

"You'd never really do that." He laughed. "I hope."

"Actually, I know you're as ready as you'll ever be. That's the only reason I'm doing this. Besides, silly boy, your associates wouldn't ever believe it, because they think you're such a straight arrow goody two-shoes."

Only the weekend remained. And after that, the trial would start.

25

Monday morning came. The courtroom was filled with broadcasters, newspaper reporters, lawyers, and curious citizens. But a central area of benches was conspicuously unoccupied.

Judge Pamela Preston looked up. "Okay, Mr. Bailiff. Bring in the jury panel."

"Yes, your honor." And a loud buzz went up from the spectators. Finally, the Emerald Rose trial was about to begin.

"Sit here, please." The deputy pointed, and the first eight citizens took their places in the front row of empty benches.

The potential jurors whispered to each other. "It's the Emerald Rose case!" . . . "This must be about the Emerald Rose!"

"It doesn't look like a good jury panel for our side," Robert Herrick whispered to Tom Kennedy.

"No, it doesn't," Tom agreed. "Too many managers and professionals. The kinds of folks who aren't sympathetic to plaintiffs' cases."

Across the courtroom, Jimmy Coleman was nodding and beaming, because this was the kind of jury panel he liked.

"This first potential juror is a grocery store manager." Robert squinted at the man's juror information form. "He's seen a thousand lawsuits, and to him, every plaintiff's claim is bogus."

"Second one's a high school teacher," Tom added. "She's heard all the sob stories."

Judge Pamela Preston smiled at the jury panel. "Good morning, ladies and gentlemen. The case now on trial involves a group of plaintiffs who are suing the Emerald Petroleum Company and other defendants."

Suddenly, the judge stopped reading instructions.

"Lawyers, please approach the bench." And a horde of attorneys hustled up.

The judge spoke quietly, so as not to be heard by the jury panel. "There's a potential juror in the third row with a T-shirt that—well, I won't say it's exactly pornographic, but it's close. And it's not appropriate for the courtroom."

Half of the lawyers had seen the sight already. They had wondered when the judge would react. The other half, now, looked at the inappropriate woman. Her T-shirt displayed a drawing of an oyster above the words, "Shuck me! Suck me! Eat me raw!," against a psychedelic background. Acquired in New Orleans, obviously, on Bourbon Street.

"I would appreciate an agreement by counsel that this potential juror is unsuitable. I can't guess which side she might be on, but I won't have that kind of message parked in my courtroom. Are we all agreed?"

"Yes, judge." "Yes, judge." "Yes, your honor." . . .

"Bailiff, please take her to the jury room, for now. I ought to hold her in contempt. But probably not. At least she showed up for jury duty, even if she's not very smart about it."

The lawyers trouped back to their places at the counsel tables.

The judge resumed her speech to the jury panel. Now, she was telling jurors not to discuss this case with anyone, including their wives and husbands.

"It's a bad jury panel," Robert whispered. "For every juror who might favor our plaintiffs, there are four who'll side with the defense."

Suddenly, a man in torn overalls stood up. "The fix is in!" He shouted. "It's all a fraud. These people aren't hurt at all."

The judge froze.

"Lawyers!" the man screamed. "They've got the President and a bunch of crooked senators behind them. Whatever these lawyers say happened, you can be sure it didn't happen!"

Now, Judge Preston reacted. "Bailiff, please remove that individual."

The prospective jurors parted like the Red Sea. The bailiff and a courtroom deputy led the deranged man out. He was yelling something about lawyers being "Muslims, and they kneel down on those toe-sacks they call prayer rugs."

"It's an omen." Tom shook his head. "This crazy man is an omen, and a bad one. Why is it that we run into this kind of luck?"

"This case has been that way for four years."

But it didn't matter. Robert knew he couldn't let it matter. He stood up to address the jury panel, with the omen of the crazy man haunting the courtroom.

* * *

In Tamaulipas, Mexico, west of Reyoso and up in the Sierra Madre Mountains, El Raton was in an expansive mood.

"You see, Charro, we are applying what is called Total Quality Management, which is known as TQM for short. We all work to satisfy our customers, all as a single team. We tell every employee to push for the product our buyers want. If they want pure stuff, that's what we supply. If it's cheaper stuff, we supply that instead."

"Yes, Jefe. Yes, my Chief. We will practice Quality Management."

"*Total* Quality Management, that is."

"Yes, Jefe. Total Quality Management. TQM."

"And the business schools say you have to knock down barriers among different departments that keep you from supplying exactly what the customer wants. That's a challenge, because we have soldiers who also are processors, and processors who occasionally are transporters."

"Yes, Jefe."

"We need everyone to understand what the customer wants right now."

"Yes, Jefe."

"There is one exception to breaking down barriers for purposes of TQM. We must still practice organizational management. With old fashioned organizational principles. We must have a single line of command, with everyone reporting to one top manager."

"And who would that be, Jefe?"

"Why, you *idiota!* Me, of course."

"Yes, yes. Of course, Jefe."

"So, we knock down anything that hinders TQM, but we keep everyone doing what I say."

"I am more than sure that will happen, Jefe."

"Now, on another subject, what about our advertising? What has happened with the orders to squash that *gusano,* that maggot, who messed up our supply chain?"

"We have put the word out, my Jefe. It is happening. More slowly than it should, probably, but it is happening."

"Hmmmm. It's happening more slowly than it should? Maybe it wouldn't hurt to practice some Total Quality Management with that job, too."

* * *

Meanwhile, many miles to the north, Robert Herrick stood and faced the jury panel. "Good morning, ladies and gentlemen. The judge told you that I am Robert Herrick, and I am. She also told you that I represent the plaintiffs in this case, and I do."

He usually started with this line. It worked. The potential jurors chuckled at the odd phrasing. By this time, jurors have sat, waited, and heard lots of instructions. Even weak humor works.

"The lawyer beside me is Francel Williams, who also represents the plaintiffs." Robert wanted to be sure to introduce Francel, who was a major presence in the black community and, in fact, in the entire community. Francel was here in his trademark pinstriped suit and silver tie.

And then, Robert turned to the first man in the panel.

"Mister Escobar." He smiled. "You are the first potential juror. You get the first questions. In fact, sometimes the first person is called the 'guinea pig juror.' Because you're the one who gets tested first."

The man laughed. "I don't do well at tests. Never did, in school."

"This isn't that kind of test. It's easier. You just answer with what you think."

"I imagine I can . . . do that." The jury panel laughed.

"Good. Now, Mr. Escobar, this is what's called a negligence case. The issue is going to be, 'Were the defendants negligent, or in other words, were they careless?' Mr. Escobar, if you hear evidence, do you think you could participate with other jurors in making a decision about negligence?"

"Sure."

"Mr. Escobar, I see that you are a grocery store manager. I reckon you have seen cases about negligence. You didn't come into the courtroom with any kind of predetermined opinion that plaintiffs should lose a negligence case, or that defendants should lose, I assume?"

"Not until I hear the evidence."

"Right. And you will hear evidence that will prove it to you. And I expect that the judge will give you a definition of negligence. It's a long definition. I expect that the judge will say something like this. *'Negligence is failing to do what a reasonable person would do, or doing what a reasonable person would not do.'* . . .

"But in ordinary language, negligence is just carelessness. Carelessness. Mr. Escobar, could you decide who was careless, based on the evidence, for whichever side had the better case?"

"Sure."

"Thank you. Now, Ms. Carey, you are the number two juror. Let me tell you what we will prove to you. We will show you two things that are very simple."

He held up one finger. "First, these defendants were very, very careless. Each of them in its own way. To use legalistic words, we expect to prove they were *negligent.* Their actions killed twenty-seven people and severely injured many more. There are more than a hundred survivors and family members, and that's who the plaintiffs are."

He looked directly at the second potential juror. "Can you decide who was negligent, in a case like that?"

"I think so, yes."

"Doctor Ermis." He focused on the third potential juror. "The second thing we will prove is that it would take more than eight hundred million dollars to compensate the plaintiffs for what they've lost." Robert paused and looked at the man. "Does that sound like a huge, enormous sum to you?"

"Well . . . yes, it sounds to me like an enormous sum!" The doctor couldn't help laughing. "Because it is."

"I know." Robert smiled. "It is. But we expect to prove to you that that's what the plaintiffs have lost. If we prove it, can you say so, if you're a juror? Is there anything that would stop you from saying so, if we prove it?"

"If you prove it."

Forty-five minutes later, Robert had asked the questions he wanted to ask. He had a sense of the potential jurors' attitudes toward his case. Only a sense, but that was all anyone ever gets from examination of jurors.

"Thank you, and thank you for being here," he said. "You are exercising a right that only free people can exercise. We sincerely appreciate your service. Thank you."

"Good job," Tom Kennedy whispered.

"Well, let's hope it was good enough for them to remember. Because next, it's Jimmy Coleman's turn. Right now. And he's going to rip it up."

26

We disagree completely with Mr. Herrick. This event was not the fault of Emerald Petroleum. It was an Act of God. It was an unavoidable accident."

Jimmy Coleman's voice sounded like the treads of a bulldozer. But he made it sound more pleasant when he turned to the first juror.

"Mr. Escobar, I noticed that Mr. Herrick acted as though someone must have been negligent. Someone. But I expect that the judge will tell you clearly, that's not the law. The law recognizes unavoidable accidents, or in other words, that things can happen that are not caused by anybody's negligence."

His voice still creaked, but now Jimmy put some honey in it. "Mr. Escobar, if this tragic event was an unavoidable accident, can you perform as an impartial juror and say so?"

"Sure."

"Thank you. Now, Ms. Carey, I see that you're a schoolteacher. I imagine you hear a lot of stories from your kids. And I imagine you have to decide whether a student is shucking you, so to speak. Or jiving you. Am I describing it accurately?"

She laughed. "Yes. Some of them can shuck and jive, both at the same time."

Jimmy laughed too, along with everyone else. "Well, Ms. Carey, as a juror you have to do the same thing. Decide whose case is true and whose isn't. Can you do that, in a case like this?"

"I think so."

"Thank you, Ms. Carey. Now . . . Doctor Ermis, this case involves a tragedy. A flat-out tragedy, and in fact a horrifying tragedy. Twenty-seven people died, and many more were injured. But the issue of who was negligent, or whether it was an unavoidable accident, or an Act of God, doesn't have anything to do with the tragedy of it."

Jimmy looked straight at the potential juror. "Dr. Ermis, can you decide whether it was an unavoidable accident, in a case that has death and terrible injuries, and ignore those injuries when you're deciding whether it was an unavoidable accident? Because that's the law."

The man frowned. "Come again? I feel like it's a strange question."

"Sure. What I'm saying is that the question about who was negligent, or whether it was an unavoidable accident, doesn't depend on how terrifying or horrible the event was. Either someone was negligent or it was an unavoidable accident. No matter what happened. My question is, can you decide whether it was an unavoidable accident without being affected by the result? Without considering how badly anyone may have been injured?"

"That's a good question."

Jimmy smiled. He was a cuddly, friendly teddy bear. "Well, see, that's the law. Doctor, we want you to be able to serve on this jury. Can you follow the law, without reference to the consequences?"

"Ahhh . . . yes, when you put it that way."

"Whether you did something wrong or not doesn't depend on the ultimate result. Doesn't that make sense?"

"Of course."

"Thank you, Doctor. Now, Ms. Geranson, you're juror number four. Ms. Geranson, I expect that you will see some disturbing pictures during this case if you serve as a juror. Our side will not impose these photographs on you during the evidence. But Mr. Herrick will. And it's important for everyone to see them ahead of time, and decide whether you can be impartial in this case."

Jimmy and his black-suited associates quickly turned over ten photographs that they had placed face down in front. The potential jurors' faces turned into masks of discomfort.

"These are the pictures of the remains of some of the poor gentlemen who died," Jimmy announced. "Their bodies are burned badly, and some of their hands and feet are missing. And there are photographs of injured men, too. I apologize for having to show these. But

Mr. Herrick has told us he plans to use them in this trial, so I feel I have to."

He faced Ms. Geranson. "Now, Ms. Geranson, you'll get these pictures during the evidence, if you are a juror. But you must not let them affect you when you decide the question of negligence, or unavoidable accident. The question I've got to ask is this. Can you do it?"

"I . . . I would try, if the judge tells me that's the law."

"Ms. Geranson, I know it's a hard question." Jimmy-the-teddy-bear emerged, and he put on his kindly smile. "But as you can see, I have to protect my client. And when you say, I would try, I understand, but it makes me get goose bumps worrying about my client. The law requires that you decide the question without considering the injuries. Think hard about whether you can do it."

"I . . . I think so."

"Thank you, Ms. Geranson. Now, I need to ask everyone in this jury panel. Is there anyone who, based on what you now know about these injuries, cannot decide the negligence or unavoidable accident question without considering the severity of the injuries?"

The result of that question was that Jimmy succeeded in having the judge remove three potential jurors, because they answered that they couldn't do it. Three citizens who might have been favorable plaintiffs' jurors.

Robert had felt optimistic about the case when he had finished his own examination of the jury panel.

But now, he no longer felt any optimism at all.

* * *

Pepper Herrick struggled to hold her head high as she trudged into the County Jail. She had discussed how to walk in with her father, as well as how to handle the rest of it.

The outer gatekeeper, and then the inner guard, buzzed her in.

Racist taunts started as soon as she was let into the dayroom. "Get out the way, you dumb honky!"

On the other hand, a few women were nicer. One of them laughed. "Don't pay no 'tention to that kinda BS. That bitch is a longtime character, well acquainted with the po-lice, and she's always mad at the whole world."

"Thank you." Pepper had prepared for it, but she was shaken.

"What brings you here?"

"Huh?"

"What do they say you did, the folks what arrested you? Don't tell me you didn't do it, because I don't care."

"Driving while intoxicated."

"Well, but gotta be more to it than that, if you done landed here."

Almost everybody wore prison whites. A few women had dresses on, wildly colored with circles and strange distorted oval shapes. Cheaply made but suitable for wearing in a courtroom.

"I got a bigger sentence because of having a wreck and an earlier DWI."

"Well, here's a piece of advice. You look too much like a princess. Try not to act like one, because that's gonna get you in trouble."

The day passed incredibly slowly. Night came. The lights never went out completely, but they dimmed to a shade that made it hard to see across the open space. You couldn't bring anything to read. Long, boring, empty hours passed, chalk-white hours, with nothing but odd conversation with strangers. Some of whom were scary because they let you know they were crazy.

The night meant that Pepper occupied the upper part of a bunk bed. She finally fell asleep after a long period of trying. There was an inmate who climbed the bars, clanking and clanking again. There was another one who sang gospel deep into the darkness.

* * *

"Jimmy, what did you have in mind?" Jennifer Lowenstein was dumbfounded. "Why did you show the jury those terrible photos at the start of the trial, when they're pictures that Robert Herrick is going to want them to see? Those pictures don't help us. They help the other side."

"Familiarity." Jimmy said it matter-of-factly. "Familiarity, and also commitment."

"Okay. That's real clear. What on earth does it mean?"

Jimmy laughed. "It's basic psychology. You've heard the old proverb that 'familiarity breeds contempt'? Well, it's not true. The experiments show that instead, familiarity breeds acceptance. People are more likely to be attracted to things or people that are familiar to them. If you don't know a given kind of music, you aren't attracted to it. But if you get to know it, you're more likely to like it."

"Well, but nobody's going to be attracted to those pictures. And these people obviously didn't appreciate having them stuck in their faces."

"But the acceptance idea still works. Something that's bad to look at becomes less of a bother when you see it a lot. The psychologists call it 'systematic desensitization.' I want the jury to feel desensitized to those pictures."

"Okay, and . . . well, I noticed that you left the photos up there the whole time. In full view."

"And I left them there after I finished, too. Desensitization."

"And also, you said something about 'commitment.' What's that got to do with it?"

"I got them to promise not to consider these pictures when they're deciding whether we were at fault. More of that basic psychology. People are more likely to do what you want them to, if they've promised you ahead of time that they'll do it."

"Not necessarily. Not always."

"Oh, I agree that it's not foolproof. People can promise you something during the jury selection and do the opposite in their verdict. But a trial gets won by a series of advantages. And I'll take this advantage, even if it doesn't come with a guarantee."

Jimmy was lecturing on a favorite subject. Just the way a visiting professor might. "Look at it this way. Those pictures are going to come into evidence. Robert Herrick will offer them, and we can argue that they ought to be excluded, but they're admissible under the rules. I'd rather have a chance to deal with them in the most favorable light possible. I'd rather not have Herrick spring them on the jurors for the first time in the middle of the trial."

27

On Sunday, Pepper Herrick left the County Jail a changed person. Not for the better.

She retrieved her clothes, purse, and personal effects. Her watch, necklace, earrings, and ring were in an envelope, together with her telephone and glasses. Everything came to her in a wire-mesh basket.

"Next time," she thought to herself, "no watch. No phone. No purse. As few clothes as possible." The experience wasn't deliberately set up for the purpose of making her feel small and worthless, but it was brutally effective at doing just that to her.

Somebody had explained it. "There have been murders inside jails, including this one, committed just to steal jewelry. So we search you, of course. Those—the murders—are cases where the deputies didn't see the jewelry, but other inmates did."

Pepper telephoned her father. Robert Herrick was waiting in his car. He picked her up at the curb, and he smiled. A forced smile, but full of relief. "Hi, my lovely daughter."

"Hi, Daddy."

Pepper was newly aware that driving while intoxicated was not desirable. Not smart. That may have been the most positive effect of this experience.

On the other hand, all of her self-confidence was gone. She felt unable to take care of herself, unable to work, unable to control herself or her life.

And she desperately wanted to go somewhere and get drunk.

* * *

Back at the federal courthouse, lawyers for Dalliman Services and Momex examined the potential jurors, just as Jimmy Coleman had. The trial became difficult to listen to, because they repeated the same themes, changed only by replacing Emerald Petroleum with their own clients' names. Robert Herrick objected repeatedly to repetitions that were too similar, tactics that went over the same ground.

There was one difference from Jimmy Coleman's examination, even though all of the defendants agreed in denying the plaintiffs' claims. These lawyers did their best to place the fault for the disaster squarely on Emerald.

And the jury examinations passed like a blur of numbing repetition.

* * *

"But I thought a jury had to have twelve people," said Randy Westhoven. He and the plaintiffs' lawyers were sitting in a meeting area by the courtroom, making their selections of jurors to strike.

"No." Robert looked at the jury information forms. "There's no fixed number, except that the Supreme Court says there have to be at least six. Federal judges usually use eight."

"Why eight, instead of ten? Or sixteen?"

"Fewer jurors shortens the trial. So judges think six is better than ten or twelve. But they add two more, in case somebody gets disqualified during the trial, so they don't have to start over."

And Robert added, "It's called jury selection, but we don't really get to select anybody. We get to remove three people, the ones we really, really don't want."

Tom spoke up. "This first potential juror, the grocery manager. He sounds evenhanded. But a grocery manager is too likely to have gotten sick of plaintiffs' claims. And this guy is decisive. He'd be a leader on the jury. Too risky."

"I liked him," said Randy Westhoven. "If we prove it, will he vote for us? His answer was, 'Sure.'"

"But Tom's right. He's the type to get the whole jury against us. We can't know for sure, of course, but it's too likely."

Randy Westhoven hesitated. Then: "Okay. You guys are experienced at this."

Robert drew a line through the man's name. This simple method was the way lawyers' strikes had been made for centuries, probably, and it was still the method today.

"Now, number two. The schoolteacher. Romanticism aside, teachers are pretty harsh in their judgments. They have to be. They say, 'This student gets an A, and this one gets an F.'"

"Yes, but she's not a leader type. Too hesitant and easily led. A follower. She wouldn't hurt us, and we've got other folks we need to get off worse."

And in this way, the lawyers worked through the jury panel. They crossed out three names.

Across the hallway, Jimmy and the other defendants were doing the same thing. They were sure to strike the potential jurors that the plaintiffs wanted the most.

"We'll end up with a jury we don't like very much," said Robert, "because we started out with a panel we didn't like very much."

"Why this case?" Tom's voice was plaintive. "This is the kind of advantage that Jimmy can use to get our injured people a bag full of nothing in the end."

*　*　*

Finally, the time came. The judge looked at Robert Herrick and said, "Call your first witness."

Who should be the first witness? "Johnny Tull," Tom Kennedy had argued. "We need someone who can set the scene. To explain what happened, overall. Johnny can do that. Johnny's a pretty solid expert. He can stand up to Jimmy Coleman and withstand cross-examination."

"Except that we have to use his formal name. Not Johnny. He sounds more like an expert if he's called John, with his middle name."

So now, Robert stood. "Your honor, the plaintiffs call John Errol Tull."

". . . Please introduce yourself to the members of the jury, Mr. Tull."

"I'm John Errol Tull, from Port Arthur, Texas."

"Mr. Tull, you are here to provide the jury with an overall picture of what happened in this blowout. And why it happened. Is that right?"

"Yes."

"I want to ask you a little bit about yourself. First of all, your middle name is Errol. Where did that come from?"

The witness chuckled. "I'm named after Errol Flynn. You know, the movie actor. He played what I would call swashbuckling roles: a ship's commander, stuff like that. And he was a screen idol. Mama liked him, and so that's where I got it."

The conventional wisdom among trial lawyers is that you help your case by telling jurors where the witness comes from and what he likes to do. There probably were at least a few jurors who knew who Errol Flynn was. To them, the witness was now, ever so slightly, a more interesting person.

For the next ten minutes, Robert led the witness through his life, starting with his elementary school, his middle school, his high school, his college years. And had he always been a Texan? "Yes sir. Never even strayed into Oklahoma." The jurors liked that answer.

John Errol Tull had a wife and three children, and Robert got him to describe them. Did he have any hobbies? "I collect guns and my wife does fancy knitting, so I guess we have all the bases covered." The jurors seemed to like that answer too.

"Now, I want to ask you about something different. What are the education, training, and experience that make you an expert about accidents on offshore platforms?"

"Out of high school, I went to work on a deep offshore platform across from Houma, Louisiana. Good job. I learned the trade from the ground up. I also made enough to put myself through college at Lamar University. I studied petroleum engineering, and I'll tell you what. I knew from my job experience that a lot of stuff in those classrooms was science fiction."

The jurors laughed. A couple of them nodded in agreement.

"Then I went back offshore as a supervisor. And then as a chief safety officer."

"Now, Mr. Tull," Robert held up his hand. "Let me change the subject again. Directing your attention to the date of the accident, do you have an opinion about why and how it happened? And if so, what is that opinion?"

"Yes. And yes. The blowout and explosion happened because of the fault of these three defendants. First, as to Emerald Petroleum. The instruments showed gas bubbling into the well. That's a sign of an impending blowout. But Emerald did not react to it. Also, Emerald used casing—that means the lining of the wellbore—that wasn't rated for this pressure.

"What about the drilling mud?"

"Yes, sir, that was something Emerald did too. Emerald's Vice President, sitting on dry land, ordered the tool pusher to replace most of the drilling mud with sea water. The tool pusher, there on the platform, he disagreed and fought against it, but the VP told him to do it anyway. The heavy drilling mud had held the pressure down, and a few minutes later, it exploded."

"Anything else that Emerald did?"

"Yes, sir. They dropped a loose pipe into the drill stem. They should have fished it immediately. Anything that impedes the line bottles up the pressure, and it's going to be more likely to blow. And maybe the worst thing of all was that Emerald created an anti-safety climate among the workers. Emerald was behind schedule, and the VP wanted to save money. The employees knew that you could lose your job if you brought up a safety issue."

Now that John Errol Tull had given his opinion, Robert had him explain it. The witness went over the sequence of events. He had been on the witness stand for three hours and had testified about nearly three hundred exhibits when Robert said, "That's all. I pass the witness."

And he braced himself for Jimmy Coleman's cross-examination.

28

Cross-examination is divided into two parts. First, you want to bring out facts favorable to your side. You want the witness to be agreeable about your points, so this is where you begin. Politely. The second part features the attack on the witness's credibility, and this part is hostile. It usually needs to be at least minimally polite, but it is a hostile kind of politeness.

And so, Jimmy was friendly at the beginning. "Mr. Witness, some people believe that fires and leaks don't happen on offshore platforms. That's wrong, isn't it?"

"Yes. Fires and leaks aren't what we want, but they can happen."

"Even with the best practices, you can't absolutely guarantee there won't be fires and leaks?"

"That's right."

"Fires and leaks are just kind of an *unavoidable* part of offshore operations, aren't they?" Jimmy buried the word that supported his theory of the case, but he would be able to read it back to the jury later, from the transcript.

"Yes, that's right. Usually, they can be taken care of, because you have all kinds of safety equipment on board the platform."

"Now, a blowout is just much bigger version of a fire and leak, isn't it?"

"I don't know if I'd . . . exactly call it a fire and leak."

"But that's what it is, isn't it? Just a bigger version of a fire and leak."

"I guess you could say that."

"And since fires and leaks are unavoidable, a blowout can be unavoidable too?" Jimmy's voice grated, but it was covered with honey.

"I reckon so, but that's what the Blowout Preventer is for."

"Exactly. And the Blowout Preventer was the responsibility of Dalliman Services, not Emerald. Not Emerald at all, right?"

"I guess so."

Two hours later, the time came for the second part of the cross-examination, Jimmy's face changed, and his voice was louder. It carried an accusing tone. He got John Errol Tull to admit he hadn't graduated from college. "I got offered a supervisor's job after my third year, and I took it."

And Tull hadn't interviewed any of the survivors who were on the platform. He knew nothing from any of the witnesses who had seen the blowout firsthand.

"Instead, you just read reports, didn't you?" Jimmy was like a boxer whose opponent was on the ropes.

"Well, yes."

"And the funny thing is, you didn't read any private reports. No industry reports. Just government reports. Right?"

"Well, yes."

"Mister Witness, you said your college courses involved a lot of science fiction." Jimmy's croak was angry, now. "Don't you think the government is capable of producing even more science fiction than your college did?"

Instantly, Robert was on his feet. "Objection, your honor. That's not proper cross-examination."

The judge sustained the objection, because Jimmy's "question" wasn't really a question, of course. But the jurors had heard it, and it probably had worked as intended. The jurors were sure to have decided that this witness's opinions were less credible than Robert had suggested.

Jimmy went on for another hour of attacks on John Errol Tull's credibility, and Robert cringed all the way through.

* * *

Pepper Herrick called in sick and spent the entire day in bed. The result was that she couldn't sleep at night. The next day, she called in sick again and slept all day. She had nightmares about being left alone, somehow, on a place that looked like a moonscape, but it was not the moon, because there were creatures that yelled racial insults at her, and she saw them in the distance, and she knew that they would kill her if they could.

"I can't call in sick again," she said to Maria Melendes. "I think they already know I'm not really sick. But the truth is, I am sick. Just not in the usual way."

"Do they know you went to jail?"

"Of course not. At least I don't think so. I haven't told anyone. And I wouldn't tell anyone except you and Jonathan and Daddy."

"Well, I'm not sure where to begin. First of all, people have all kinds of different reactions to the inside of a jail. Some people just go through it as something they have to do. At the opposite extreme, there are people who develop mental illnesses."

"That sounds like me."

"No, not at all. Your reaction is better than a lot of people."

"I'd hate to see someone who was worse off."

"Believe me, it's true. You'd hate to see what jail does to some people."

"What do I do?"

"First thing, and this is a judgment call, think about whether it makes sense to tell your boss. I have to add, it may not always be wise. Some people are narrow-minded. But you'd be surprised. Usually, they're sympathetic."

"Really? You think so?"

"They think you're a good employee, don't they? They think you do a good job?"

"They always tell me so."

"I'd tell them about going to jail. I'd just tell them."

"I don't know. I just don't know."

* * *

"Call your next." Judge Pamela Preston looked at Robert.

"The plaintiffs call Randall Westhoven."

Once on the witness stand, Randy Westhoven blinked. He looked disoriented. Robert immediately thought to himself, "Ooops. I should have brought this man into the courtroom before the trial started and had him sit in the witness chair. In an empty courtroom."

Some witnesses feel better, that way, when they testify. They're more confident if they've been inside the courtroom beforehand and sat in the witness chair. And without it, they may be discombobulated when they're called as witnesses.

"Would you state your name for the members of the jury, please?"

"Randall Westhoven."

"You usually go by Randy?"

". . . Randy. Yes." The witness was hesitant about even saying his name.

"Randy, you are one of the plaintiffs and are here to tell the jury about your loss. Is that right?"

"Yes."

"Who was it that you lost?"

"My daddy. He was a supervisor, and he was near the derrick at the time of the explosion. His body was burned completely." Randy Westhoven's eyes glistened. "We had a memorial service, but we couldn't have an open casket. At least we were able to bury him in the plot that he had reserved, next to my mother. His wife of nearly forty years."

Robert looked at his lead plaintiff. "Do you need to take a break, Randy?"

". . . No, thank you." The witness visibly pulled himself together.

Sometimes, if an attorney asks this question of a struggling witness, it gives the witness an impression that he has at least a little control of the situation. Even if the answer is no. Robert paused for a moment and pretended to look over his notes to give the witness time.

"Tell the jury what your father was like when you were growing up."

In this way, Robert took the witness through his life. And his father's. After something between a half hour and forty-five minutes, he said, "I pass the witness."

Jimmy Coleman was ready. "Good afternoon, Mr. Westhoven."

"Ahhh . . . good afternoon."

"You have painted a picture of a close relationship with your father. But we asked during discovery for any pictures in your possession showing you doing any activity with your father, and you don't have a single picture. Is that right?"

"Yes. I have pictures of him doing things and me doing things that he taught me to do, such as riding a bicycle."

"But not a single one of you and your father together doing the activities that you now claim were so frequent."

"No."

"And at the time of his death, I believe you told us in your deposition that you saw him maybe twice a year."

"Maybe."

Jimmy kept Randy Westhoven on the witness stand for over an hour testifying about pictures he didn't have, records he didn't have, and activities he'd never done with his father.

Robert felt a hole in his stomach as he and Tom left the courtroom. "How badly did we lose with Randy Westhoven?"

"He was pretty nervous. And his personality didn't come across at all." Tom frowned. "Another reason to remember that ... well, we could have tried harder to settle this case."

29

It was Saturday morning when Maria Melendes called. Robert was in the middle of witness preparation for next week, but Donna deCarlo was insistent. "I think you'd better stop what you're doing and talk to her."

So he excused himself and went to another telephone. "Hi, Maria. What's up? What's so urgent?"

"It's Pepper. Again."

"Oh, no. What is it this time? Did she not show up for weekend service of her sentence? The court will revoke the weekend arrangement and make her serve it all right away."

"No. It's worse than that."

"What is it, then? What?"

"She showed up for weekend service, but she showed up drunk."

"Oh, no."

"Jonathan brought her there, like a good husband, right on time. But he couldn't un-drunk her."

"What will happen to her now?" Robert was thinking wild thoughts about how bad it might be.

"Well, nothing's going to happen right now. On Sunday, she'll stay over. I mean, she'll still be in jail after she's supposed to be released. She'll be held on a commitment-type warrant, sort of as if she'd just been arrested. She'll spend an extra night, Sunday night. And then, she'll go to court on Monday morning to see the judge, and he can revoke her weekend service."

"Oh, no."

"Well, the good thing is, she's already been sentenced, so she can't get more jail time. When Monday starts, she'll have done three days. So: Monday, Tuesday, Wednesday. I guess if the judge decides to revoke weekend service, she'll be back out Wednesday evening."

"Better call her lawyer for Monday morning."

"Right. I've put in a call. It's not going to be easy reaching him on Saturday, but I'll get him sooner or later."

"We'd better also call her boss on Monday. And tell him she had another attack of the flu."

"Okay. I hate it. But yes, we'll have to do that."

"She should've just explained to her boss about getting arrested. You told her to do that. I did too. Now it's too late. Instead of coming clean about it, she took the easy way and did nothing. She'd rather keep pretending. She'd rather keep lying."

"It proves the old saying about kids and happiness, doesn't it?"

"What old saying?"

"An old saying that goes like this: 'You can never be happier than your unhappiest kid.'"

They both laughed at that. But the saying was true, and it was a sad laugh. It was the kind of laugh you laugh when you tell yourself there's nothing else to do but laugh.

* * *

Robert couldn't be in the Criminal Courts Building with Pepper on Monday morning. He was across town in the Federal Building, appearing before Judge Preston and the jury.

"Call your next." The judge said it mechanically.

Robert stood. "Your honor, the plaintiffs call Alphonse Hebert."

The witness was rough-looking, weathered and sunburned, and wearing a brown polyester jacket with a brown tie. He spelled his name, asked to be called "Al," and told the jury how his last name was pronounced ("AY-bear"). "It's a good, solid Cajun name."

And then, Robert got down to business.

"You are here to tell this jury about the blowout and explosion, because you were the alternate tool pusher on the platform, right?"

"That's right. Dere were t'ree tool pushas, one fo each shift. I was one of dem."

"What is a 'tool pusher'? It's a familiar word in the oil patch, but please tell the jury what it means."

"Simple. De tool pusha is de supervisa at de oil derrick." The witness had more than a Cajun name; he also had a fierce Cajun accent. "De tool pusha watches ovah de roughnecks what do de woik of drillin. I was a roughneck fo' twenty-odd yeahs mahself, befo' this."

"Now, Al, did there come a day when you had a disagreement with the Vice President of Production for Emerald Petroleum?"

"It did."

"Please tell us about that. What was the disagreement about?"

"De VP told me, drain half of dat mud dat's in de drill stem and put in sea water. Dat woulda had de well going fastah. But I was convinced that de mud was what was holding de pressure down. I been in blowouts befo'. It's dangerous as all get out."

"But he told you to do it anyway."

"Dat's right."

"What, in your judgment, caused the blowout and explosion?"

"Exactly dat. De sea water couldn't hold like de drillin mud, 'cause de drillin mud is heavy. It's made fo' dat."

The witness paused and said, "And I know dat's what it was, 'cause de well blew up right while we were replacin de mud."

"It didn't take a lot of down-home Cajun logic to figure that out, I guess."

"In Southern Louisiana, we woulda called it coon-ass thinkin." The witness smiled. A second later, all of the jurors laughed, and so did the judge. Even though use of the term by outsiders is disfavored, a genuine Louisiana coon-ass can call himself a coon-ass.

"But the VP didn't agree with you."

"I c'n tell you, we din't agree at all. I yelled at him on de phone. I used some choice cuss words. I told him it was gonna kill us all. He just said de same ting, every time, about how de well was way behind schedule."

Robert led Al Hebert through the other causes of the blowout—the gas bubbling into the drill stem, the casing that was inadequate, the pipe that dropped into the well, and the company's creation of an anti-safety culture—and then, he concentrated on the explosion itself.

"I tell you, it was like a piece'a de sun fell down on dis platform." The witness was serious, now. "It was dat bright, dat hot. It lasted what seemed forrr-ever. And den, dere was a whole passel of unrecognizable people, all blackened an' miss-shaped, and dere was guys burnin all over who ran and jumped off de edge and inta de ocean."

The direct examination of Al Hebert lasted an hour and a half before Robert said, "I pass the witness."

* * *

Jimmy Coleman got straight to the point when he started his cross-examination.

"If the Blowout Preventer had worked, there wouldn't have been any blowout, would there?"

"No. Dat's what de Blowout Preventer is fowah."

"And Emerald Petroleum didn't have any responsibility for the Blowout Preventer, right?"

"Dat's right."

"Now, Mr. Hebert, being the tool pusher is actually a pretty big job, because you have so many people to supervise. Don't you?"

"It's de biggest job I evah had."

"You're in charge of everyone in the area, no matter which company originally hired them."

"Dat's right."

"And even if someone got their paycheck from Dalliman or Momex or Amadanko, they really worked under you when they were on the platform, right?"

"Dat's right."

"Every worker there was really borrowed by Emerald Petroleum from Dalliman and Momex and Amadanko, and they were just like Emerald employees. They were borrowed servants of Emerald under your supervision, weren't they?"

"Dat's right."

When Jimmy passed the witness, the lawyers for Dalliman and Momex fell all over themselves pointing out that even before the Blowout Preventer failed, Emerald Petroleum had engaged in enough dangerous, foolish, negligent acts so that the Blowout Preventer couldn't possibly have been expected to hold back the pressure.

And both of them tried to show that when their employees weren't standing right beside the derrick, they had separate duties—duties that weren't under Emerald's control, so that they weren't borrowed servants.

"I like seeing these defendants fighting over which one's at fault," Tom said, as they walked out of the courtroom. "They're all pointing at each other."

"Yes," said Robert. "It feels good for a change. But it can backfire, and then it can turn out badly for us. Jimmy seems to be getting ahead in that fight, and we'll be in trouble if he wins it in the end."

30

Back at the Herrick home, Pepper had news.

"So you told your boss about going to jail? And you didn't get fired?" Robert was relieved. Probably more so about her having the ability to admit it than about her keeping this particular job.

"Yes. I was really scared to tell him."

And he could see that she was also scared to tell her Daddy about it. So he said, "A lot of life involves doing scary things that need to be done."

"I guess."

"What did he say, your boss?"

"He said, he understood. But there were two conditions on my going back to work. The first one was that I can't do it ever again. Get arrested for intoxicated driving, I mean. The second one, he said, was something I needed to do so that I could do the first thing. And that is, I have to participate in AA. Alcoholics Anonymous."

"Sounds . . . sensible to me."

"Except that I'm not an alcoholic. I drank more than I should have a couple of times. I'm going to do it, yes, but only because I want my job. I'm not an alcoholic. I know myself, and I'm just not an alcoholic."

"Well." Robert didn't believe her, but it seemed foolish to argue. "Well, yes. Do it."

* * *

The next morning, the Emerald Rose trial ground on. It already seemed to have lasted forever, but everyone knew it had a long way to go.

Francel Williams was in charge of the next witness. A labor economist. He would be on the witness stand for an entire day, if not longer.

"Doctor," Francel began, "I'd like to ask you, first of all, what the usual reaction of listeners is, to the kind of testimony you're about to give. How is the jury likely to feel about it?"

The witness smiled. "People usually think the information from a labor economist is dense, mathematical, and excruciatingly boring. Really boring, people usually say."

Francel wore his inevitable striped suit and silver tie. The witness looked like the professor he was, with thick black-framed glasses, white hair, and a herringbone jacket that had suede elbow patches.

"Well, the jury will be asked about monetary earnings and so forth. Why, then, are we about to bore them so badly?"

The jurors let out a doubtful sounding laugh. But at least they laughed.

"The plaintiffs have to present this kind of evidence," the witness answered. "Otherwise, the jury would have no basis for figuring this part of the damages, which will be one of the questions they'll have to answer."

"So. Having told the jury that, which probably isn't good news to any of them," Francel grinned, "let's get started so we can get it done."

"Yes, sir." Francel and Robert were both glad to see that the jurors were amused by this warning at the beginning. Now, they could hope that the testimony wouldn't turn these good citizens off, even though it might put them to sleep.

"Doctor, let me start by asking you about Randy Westhoven's father. Sanford J. Westhoven. He called himself Sandy Westhoven, and he was one of those who died in the explosion. Doctor, did you do a projection of earnings for him?"

"Yes."

"Doctor, were you able to project what the total dollar value would have been, of his past earnings to date since death plus his future earnings, if he had not been killed in this disaster?"

"Yes. I estimate the total dollar value to be eleven million, five hundred thousand dollars."

"And can you please tell us how you arrived at this figure?"

"It involved several steps. First, I figured out his life expectancy. Which isn't difficult, because it is published by the federal government. Second, I estimated his probable working life. Then, third, I was able to use his record of earnings during lifetime to project his probable earnings after death, if he had lived to his life expectancy. "

"And that last step—using his record of earnings—how is that done?"

"It is a multiple-step process itself. He could reasonably have anticipated increases in earnings. Partly from pure inflation. Partly from advancement. The record during his lifetime was the baseline for that."

"Thank you. Now, eleven and a half million is the total, you say. But the jury has to find the present value of that amount. The value of that spread-out eleven and a half million dollars, if it were all paid today. What would that be?"

"I can project that the present value of the eleven and a half million would be an estimated eight million dollars."

"And doctor, please tell us how this figure was computed. . . ."

The testimony droned on, in this way.

Finally, Francel had the witness identify a chart that, for every dead or injured person, gave total figures and present values. That was what the jurors would ultimately fasten onto, the plaintiffs hoped.

The chart was important because the jurors' eyes were completely glazed over even though this was an early part of the doctor's testimony. It was, certainly, evidence that was dense, mathematical, and excruciatingly boring, just as promised.

After the labor economist had thoroughly discussed the earnings picture for Sanford J. Westhoven, Francel moved on to the next plaintiff. And after that, to the next. Each one involved explaining the same kind of mathematical calculations for another dead or injured worker.

* * *

Friday night came. And with it, a little time off. In fact, this Friday night was a time for silliness.

Every lawyer would love to be an actor. Law students are attracted to the profession partly because they believe—wrongly, they will discover—that law school will teach them how to perform smoothly in a courtroom. Anyway, the desire to act stays with them. Bar associations everywhere produce plays and musicals featuring their members.

In this city, lawyers certainly had the opportunity to become actors. The annual musical presented by the Bar Association was called *Night Court*. It had a long and rollicking history.

Tonight, Robert Herrick was backstage. He heard one question, repeated by everyone he saw. "How can you find the time to do this show, with that huge trial going on?"

"The judge supports *Night Court*," he told them all. "She's helped me with scheduling. And I've got to have something like this to do, or I'd go crazy."

He also told some of them, "I figured out you have to plan things like this in your personal life, the same way you plan your time practicing law. You actually have to schedule your personal life. Or else, you won't have a personal life, because the law will swallow it up."

The past *Night Courts*, in earlier years, had carried colorful names, like "Viva Laws Vegas" or "Laws in Space"—names patterned after well-known productions, but with the word "Laws" inserted. The show had earned hundreds of thousands of dollars, all donated to charity.

This year, the title was "Words of Law." The show opened with the whole cast singing the theme song, which was based on a hit song from the 1960's. The scene featured three-part harmony, with Robert among the dozen voices carrying the tune:

> Words of Law . . . of-ficially printed,
> Won't win the court's heart any more.
> You wanta use law? You gotta bend it
> To where it doesn't look like what it was before.
> Twisted phrases, and verbal crazes,
> Can get you where you want to go. . . .

And the show went on, with parodies like this one, for nearly three hours. When the curtain came down, Robert was exhausted, like all the other players.

But at least he'd had three hours that took his mind off the Emerald Rose case.

*   *   *

Monday morning came. And with it, a witness with a dramatic picture to draw, if he could only express it.

"It was really undescribable. I can't even tell you about it. Ugly. A horror picture."

Tom Kennedy had this witness. He had found the man: a Coast Guard lieutenant named Isaac Massad. And now, Tom was presenting him to the jury.

But Isaac Massad wasn't a very good storyteller. "Lieutenant, please tell us what you saw."

"It was horrible. No way I can explain."

"All right. Let's back up. Your helicopter flew to a well tender vessel. On board, there were the worst injured, from the first life raft off the Emerald Rose. This vessel just happened by?"

"Yes. That's it. The worst injured. Triaged to be salvageable, but inside that group, the ones hurt worst. They put them into the first lifeboat."

"This was how long after the explosion began, when your helicopter arrived at the tender vessel?"

"Can't be sure. More than seven hours."

"And the people you saw included one gentleman with an injured neck."

"More than just injured. He had burns on his chest, his face, his arms. He had a long deep cut across his neck, and he was screaming. Low vitals. We thought we'd lose him. Screaming from the pain, all that time later. All we could do was to put him into a cradle, tried not to jostle him but we did jostle him, and have him lifted. There's morphine up in the helo. And antibiotics and other stuff."

"Other injured people?"

"There was one guy with a tourniquet and a huge bandage over his hand, or what was left of it. His bones showed. Burnt bones. There were blisters all over him and charred skin on his arms and his body. He was screaming too."

The witness wiped his eyes. The jurors were fascinated and repulsed at the same time. They wore frowns and quizzical looks, and all of them stared at Isaac Massad.

When the nightmare description was over and Tom passed the witness, everyone expected Jimmy Coleman to pass the witness too and say, "No questions." But that wasn't Jimmy's style.

"You can't tell us that these individuals didn't recover, can you?" he wanted to know.

And Jimmy ended with, "But anyway, you're not saying that any of this was Emerald Petroleum's fault, are you? Because you weren't there in time to have any kind of judgment about that, right?"

31

The parade of witnesses continued in the Emerald Rose case.

Today was autopsy day, and the witness was the Chief Medical Examiner. His name was entirely unpronounceable from its spelling. He was Doctor Bill Brczykowski.

But the name Brczykowski actually was easy, the witness explained. "BAR-chee-KOW-ski." In spite of the gloom that should have dominated his profession, he favored the jurors with a brilliant smile.

"Even so," said Robert with a smaller smile, "people call you by a shorter name. Don't they, Doctor BAR-chee-KOW-ski?"

"Yes. I'm known as 'Doctor Bill' for short." Another big smile. "But I can't imagine why."

The jurors liked that. Robert played along. This tall, gaunt forensic pathologist habitually amused himself and onlookers by feigning surprise at the difficulty people had with the spelling of his name.

"Would you tell the jury, please, what a 'Medical Examiner' does?"

"Certainly. In many places, the Medical Examiner is known as the 'Coroner.' The biggest part of the job is determining the cause of death whenever there are unusual circumstances."

Doctor Bill BAR-chee-KOW-ski was a colorful sight. He sported a green and white plaid jacket with a large, wide pattern, a tan button-down shirt, and a green bow tie with white polka dots. His trousers were a matching green, with crisp pleats; and he wore white socks that ended brightly in white patent shoes. His coke-bottle glasses and white beard made him look like an expert, and so did his white hair, parted in the middle.

The good Doctor told the jurors about his medical school, internship, and residency, and then about his publications, teaching, and experience. Some of the jurors blinked. It was hard to tell whether they were impressed with Doctor BAR-chee-KOW-ski's credentials or just shielding their eyes from his wardrobe.

"Doctor," Robert asked more seriously, "did your office perform an autopsy on the body of Sanford J. Westhoven, the father of Randy Westhoven?"

"Yes."

"And Doctor, what was your opinion of the cause of death?"

Doctor Brczykowski flashed the same lighthouse smile. "Asphyxiation and cardiac arrest!" He said it with disarming enthusiasm.

"How would that be the cause of death, Doctor, when the body was fully covered by blackening burns on the outside?"

"The lungs take in gases and air." The witness still had his incongruous grin as he faced the jury. "But then the lungs burn and they cannot absorb the oxygen. Asphyxiation. The heart quickly stops for the same reason."

"Would these injuries be painful, for the time it takes for death or unconsciousness to result?"

"Yes, extremely so. The body would go into shock quickly, but there is a period of time."

"Now, Doctor, I need to take you through the autopsy. What did you see externally?"

"The body was that of a well-formed, apparently healthy male in his fifties. The skin had been entirely engulfed in flames. Separately, the identity of this individual had been determined by dental records. The testes were not palpable in the scrotum because of rigor mortis and burns."

Every autopsy report, Robert thought to himself, contains remarks on this odd subject: on whether the testes were, or were not, palpable in the scrotum. Always, if the decedent is male. For some reason known only to pathologists, the observation seems to be mandatory.

So, Robert went on to say, "Thank you, Doctor Bill. Now: did you start the internal autopsy in the normal way?"

"Yes. We began with the usual Y-shaped incision at the abdomen, which gave access to the organs. The heart, lungs, and liver all were removed and weighed."

"And the head?"

"We reflected the head in the usual way." The Doctor turned to the jury, still with a toothy smile. "That means that we cut around the crown with a saw designed for the purpose, removed the cranial cap, and extracted the brain."

A few jurors wrinkled their noses at that, but they did not appear nauseated enough to lose their judgment. And juries seem to respond better in death cases if they hear something about what happens during the autopsy. So again, Robert went on.

"Were the organs normal?"

"Yes, except for the lungs."

Robert had a photograph marked with a number. He offered it into evidence after having the witness identify it. "The exhibit is a photograph of the body of Sanford J. Westhoven at the time we began the autopsy," said Doctor Bill. "The exhibit correctly shows its condition at that time."

"Your honor," said Robert, "I offer this Plaintiff's exhibit into evidence."

"It's admitted," said Judge Preston.

The bailiff projected the photograph onto the courtroom screen. It showed an object the color of a lump of coal, barely recognizable as a human body.

There was a loud gasp from the jury box. And from the courtroom in general. The jurors had seen this photograph together with others during jury selection, because Jimmy had shown it then. But knowing about the person made the photograph more shocking.

"Thank you, Doctor," Robert said quietly. "Now, I would like to ask you about another individual, namely, Gerald Hanna. And let me add, for the benefit of the jury, that we will be able to cover the rest of the autopsies in less time than this first one. I know it's unpleasant."

But if it was unpleasant, the beaming expression worn by Doctor BAR-chee-KOW-ski did not show it. Well, Robert said to himself, death was the good Doctor's subject of interest—and, obviously, for him, it was a subject of happy fascination.

* * *

Down in Tamaulipas, Mexico, El Raton was also thinking about death. But his interest in the subject was different from Doctor Brczy-kowski's.

"Charro," he said angrily, "we have lost another shipment."

"No, Jefe. No. I cannot believe it."

"We are doing well in our business, overall. The losses have been a small percentage of our sales, so far. But the percentage has grown. And sooner or later, it will affect our balance sheet and our profit-and-loss statement."

"I know, Jefe. And although we cannot afford to care about the individuals arrested with the seizure of the shipment, new couriers are becoming more expensive. They see the trade as risky to them."

"Which is cowardly on their parts. They should go ahead and work for us without regard to the risk."

"Yes. That is why we should not care about them now, even if they decay and die in prison."

"We had a more efficient supply chain at an earlier time, when we were using the Emerald Rose as a transshipment point. And then this maggot from the *Estados Unidos* called the Coast Guard. We haven't done anything about that yet."

"Jefe, we have contracted the job of sending a message about that. But apparently, it has been more difficult than usual to kill that particular maggot—that individual named Tom, in the United States."

"I want it done." Suddenly El Raton was angrier still. "I want it done! Get in touch with our functionaries in the United States. Tell them we want it done, or there will be consequences."

* * *

A thousand miles north, in Judge Pamela Preston's courtroom, the Case of the Emerald Rose lurched into yet another week.

Robert stood to address the court. "Your honor, the plaintiffs call Doctor Enrique Pena. Our geophysicist."

Doctor Pena explained what a geophysicist did. "The name sounds like a combination of a geologist and a physicist, and that's basically correct. In the oil field, a geophysicist knows how to identify formations below ground and to figure out their contents, pressure, and depth."

"Doctor Pena, are you familiar with the geophysics of the Emerald Rose platform at the time of the event that is in question in this case?"

"Yes. I have studied the well logs and other documents that reflect the formations and conditions below the sea bed at that time."

"What conclusions did you reach?"

"First, removal of the drilling mud from the drill stem and replacement by sea water meant that a blowout was likely. The pressure of natural gas at the well bottom exceeded the pressure per square inch that could be counterbalanced by sea water in the drill stem. Second, the Blowout Preventer was inadequate to hold that pressure. Third, the casing on the drill stem was also inadequate."

"Did you reach any conclusion, Doctor Pena, about the fact that gas was bubbling into the well stem?"

"Yes. That is an important indicator of a potential impending blowout."

"Would you say that the Blowout Preventer being inadequate and the other inadequacies were concurrent causes?"

Jimmy was on his feet. "Objection, your honor. Leading question."

"Let me rephrase that question," said Robert immediately. "Doctor Pena, did you conclude anything with respect to concurrent causes?"

"Yes. The inadequacy of the Blowout Preventer operated together with the other defects to cause the blowout and explosion. They were concurrent causes."

When he completed his testimony with explanations of the scientific methods that supported his conclusions, Doctor Enrique Pena looked like a solid, persuasive witness.

"Good job," said Tom Kennedy to Robert.

"I hope so." Robert kept his expression even. "But next, we'll hear from Jimmy, and I bet he'll have something to say during cross-examination."

32

J immy started his cross-examination with a bang.

"Mister Pena, how much are you being paid per hour to testify for the plaintiffs?"

The witness seemed startled by the grinding tone of Jimmy's voice. "Ahhh," he said, and paused. Finally, he answered, ". . . Four hundred dollars per hour."

"And by now, you've spent hundreds of hours on this job."

"I don't know exactly."

"Each hundred hours you spend, multiplied by four hundred dollars, means an additional forty thousand dollars right there in your pocket, doesn't it?"

"I haven't done the math, to be honest."

At that, Jimmy stood, with a puzzled expression. And he walked to the blackboard in the courtroom.

"All right, Mister Expert, let's do the math. If I write $ 400 here, that's the amount you get every hour. And let's multiply that by 100. Just like we learned to do in elementary school. And what's the total? The result?"

The witness stared at the blackboard. "Ahhh . . . forty thousand."

"Forty thousand dollars. Correct. So, wouldn't you agree with me, that for every hundred hours you spend on this case, you earn . . . *forty thousand dollars?*"

"Well . . . yes."

"Now, let me ask you this. Should the jury put any faith in a so-called scientific expert who needed to get someone to explain elementary school math to him at the blackboard, like I did just now?"

Robert stood immediately. "I object, your honor. That's a highly improper question."

"Sustained," said Judge Preston just as immediately.

"Well, let me ask a question you can answer," said Jimmy indifferently. His voice sounded like hailstones in a bamboo field. "What are you paid per year in your usual job, as a professor at Rice University?"

"A hundred and thirty-five thousand dollars per year."

"So, assuming a forty hour workweek, that would be about fifty dollars an hour. Right?"

"I'll take your word for it."

"In other words, at four hundred dollars an hour, here, you're making nearly ten times as much money as you make in your regular job."

"I suppose."

"And who was it, who offered you this princely sum per hour? Who on the plaintiff's side made that agreement with you?"

"The lawyer who I worked with, who asked me questions here. Mister Robert Herrick."

"Mister Pena." Jimmy carefully avoided addressing the man as "Doctor" or "Professor," and he delivered his words with sledgehammer heaviness. "Mister Pena. For forty thousand dollars per hundred hours, don't you suppose you might be tempted to shade the truth in favor of the plaintiffs just a little bit? Or actually, more than a little bit?"

"Not at all," was the witness's answer. But he sounded weak. Indecisive.

And biased.

When Jimmy went on to question the witness about the disaster itself—Wasn't it true that the Blowout Preventer was inadequate? And if it had been substantial enough to prevent the blowout, wouldn't you agree that we wouldn't even need to be here in court today?—Doctor Enrique Pena answered in a voice so shaky that he didn't seem to know the answers.

And Robert realized that his expert geophysicist, who had seemed so solidly persuasive just a few moments before, was no longer impressive at all.

* * *

Later, when the sun was down and the sky was dark, Robert steered into the driveway beside the sign that said, "Sunrise Green Assisted Living. This Is Your Home."

And he walked slowly to the door that said, "Rosalie Herrick."

"Hi, Mama. Mama Rosalie." He had trouble calling her by her first name, even though she insisted.

"Hi, Robert." She knew him this time. Her awareness varied; it came and went.

But she seemed unusually thoughtful about something.

"What is it, my Mama?"

"Oh, it's Sarah. My friend Sarah. She transferred to the hospital today. This afternoon. Or maybe it was this morning."

He paused and looked at her. "I know you're worried. You talk about Sarah a lot."

"Yes. One of the servants here, I mean one of the assistants, was talking, and I heard him. And he said, 'It looks like the end.'"

"I'm . . . sorry."

"I will miss her." She looked away. When she looked back, it was with her usual mood. A happier mood. "What did you do today, Robert?"

"I was in court. Honestly, it didn't seem to go well."

"In court? I worry about you in court. Are you going to have to go to jail?"

He had to struggle to keep from laughing. "No. Jail isn't the problem. The problem is that I'm the lawyer for people who are hurt badly and I feel like they're losing. Because of me."

"Well, it just won't do for you to go around exaggerating your importance that way." She smiled at him.

At that, he laughed.

She smiled, but she was serious. "Robert, our family always takes responsibility. It's one of the things I admired about my Frederick. Your Daddy. It's a good thing, taking responsibility. But you can carry it too far."

He looked at her and waited.

And he remembered why he was here. It wasn't just a duty. She was interesting. She was surprising. And she asked him questions that he didn't know how to answer.

"Besides," she said finally, "when we take too much responsibility, we almost always make things look worse than they are."

"I . . . guess so."

"Is that what you're doing? Exaggerating what you think are your mistakes and deciding that you're losing? That's not good."

". . . May . . . maybe."

"When I feel that way, I stop and ask myself, what if I'm wrong and it's actually going better than I've been thinking? And I think of the reasons it could be true."

"I don't want to fool myself."

"No." She spoke abruptly. "Don't do that. But the idea is, you don't know yet. And you have to think both ways. Including the optimistic way. If you do that, you're more likely to make it turn out right."

He stared at her. She always surprised him.

An hour later, driving home, he puzzled over what she had said and what it meant. I think this trial is going badly, he told himself. I have to keep that in mind, the idea that it's going badly, because I don't want to fool myself. But I have to be optimistic. And I can't seem to do that. Because I'm losing, in fact. But I have to make myself feel optimistic. And at the same time, I have to remember the possibility that it's going badly.

I wonder, he said to himself, whether I should have chosen to become a trial lawyer.

*   *   *

The Case of the Emerald Rose lurched into its ninth week.

Robert called more plaintiffs to the witness stand, the ones who had not yet testified. And more doctors to testify about the injuries of the survivors.

And more expert witnesses to testify about pain and suffering from burns, about proper ways to handle a well that when it reaches depth, and about the earnings of the dead and injured.

And wives, to testify about the loss of companionship from their departed or badly injured husbands.

Finally, it was time to call the last witness. Who happened also to have been the first witness. Robert called Randy Westhoven to the witness stand once again.

"Randy, you've been here next to me during this entire trial. You've heard Mr. Coleman say several times that injuries and losses of the plaintiffs are exaggerated. In your case, what do you think of that?"

"It's disturbing that he suggests that." This answer had been carefully rehearsed, partly so that it wouldn't sound rehearsed. "My loss of my Daddy isn't exaggerated. Not by a long shot. If anything, it's understated. I can't adequately explain it. My ability to use words to explain a loss like this isn't up to the job, and it's a much bigger thing than I can explain."

"And in the course of this trial and the lead-up to it, you've come to know others of the plaintiffs. Are they exaggerating their losses and injuries, the way Mr. Coleman claims they are?"

Jimmy objected immediately. "Not the kind of opinion that can be given by a witness who is not an expert."

"Sustained," said the judge.

But the jury had heard the question and had seen Jimmy Coleman object to a description of his trial tactics. Good.

Jimmy Coleman's questions were short. Did Mr. Westhoven remember his earlier testimony? Did he recall saying that he was unable to produce any pictures of him and his father doing any activities together? Or anything that could show that his father gave him any advice?

"Well, then, since you have no photographs and no indication of advice, don't you have to admit that the loss of your father is less damaging than it might be if you had those things?"

"No." By now, Randy Westhoven was accustomed to the courtroom, and his voice was angry. "No, not at all. Mr. Coleman, you live in a fantasy world."

Robert watched with satisfaction as Jimmy thought about objecting to the unresponsive part of this answer—and ended his cross-examination instead.

Robert stood and addressed the judge. "Your honor, the plaintiffs rest."

Finally, the plaintiffs' part of the Emerald Rose Case was over.

33

Maria, Baby, you're always dragging me to art museums, even during a long trial. You sure do love these art museums."

The Menil Museum is oddly located. It sits in the middle of a residential neighborhood, and from a block away, it looks more like an elementary school than an art museum. Robert and Maria walked past a sign that said, *Picasso: The Line*.

"Well, but Robert . . . you got to sleep late this morning." Maria Melendes laughed. "You have a week off. You can be a good guy for one afternoon, since the judge has recessed the trial."

"Great. But actually, I'm a good guy all the time, aren't I? Or most of the time?"

"Yes. You're good to the courts. You're good to your associates and partners. And especially, you're good to your clients."

She laughed again. "Now, it's time to be good to *me*. Your wife."

"Okay. But I don't always care for Picasso." Robert was still unhappy about spending his time this way.

"I don't either." Maria's answer was cheerful. "But Picasso's stuff is almost always challenging. I guess all of these works feature interesting lines."

He laughed. "Since the title is *Picasso: The Line*, I hope it has something to do with lines. I'll be happy if all of them are as interesting as you say."

The first featured work was called *Violin on a Table*. It showed blue, brown, and gray shapes crossed by black lines, all on a mottled cream background. Robert perked up. "Okay. This one is interesting."

"Why do you say that? Because I know, I know—with you, there has to be a complicated reason. Robert Herrick can't just *like* a piece of art."

He laughed again. "That's right, I guess. Just to make it overly intellectual, I'd say that the lines are rhythmical, but they're different. See, there are four prominent lines that repeat, sort of in parallel. Artists call that 'rhythm,' when things on the canvas are related to each other like that. But this second line is zigzagged, and this third one makes a slightly different angle, so that they create variations. And yet the relationship among the lines is clear. And this other set of softer lines is also rhythmical, but it leans in the opposite direction."

"Okay, Mister Art Critic. Only, I hope you won't talk in the same complicated way when it comes to talking to the jury in your big case."

"Oh, no! I hope I won't make that mistake." But he knew he needed to pay attention to what she was saying.

"Besides," she added, "it sounds like it would be easy to draw this piece. You just set up four lines leaning in one direction and four lines going in the other direction."

"Keep saying 'it sounds' easy, because it's not easy at all. To make them not quite parallel but make them pleasingly proportioned—no, that's not easy at all."

"Okay. It's 'pleasingly proportioned'? But here's my question. Why do you like this particular piece of art?"

"Well, there's also a relationship between the solid objects and these disembodied lines drawn across the sheet. There's this blue violin, and this brown table. And the gray floor. But the colors complement each other, in spite of being a novel combination. This is what they call Cubism, meaning that the artist shows multiple views of the solid shapes from different directions at the same time."

"I hope, Mister Art Critic, that you really struggle to keep from talking to the jury this way, because their eyes are going to glaze over."

"Okay." He laughed. "Here's a simple thought. I like art that's in color, instead of plain old drawings with just black and white. Is that the right way to talk to a jury?"

"Ah. So, inside that imaginative art theoretician, there's actually a kid named Robert who is still stuck in elementary school. Who likes cartoons, but only if they're in color." She laughed too—and then turned serious. "But yes, that's better way to talk to a jury. Simple and straightforward."

"I guess so. Now, this next drawing is one that I don't like. This one is called *Sketch of Andre Salmon*. It's a work in Cubism, and the nose is seen from a different point of view from the eyes. But the lines aren't interesting. They go in all directions, with no rhythm."

"So it's all right to say, 'It would be easy to draw this one?'"

He laughed. "Yes. More so than the one with the blue violin."

Later, when they stopped at the Menil Bistro for coffee, he marveled at how much better he felt about this museum visit than he had expected. He and Maria made each other laugh.

And he found himself turning over in his mind what she had said. She was right about how to talk to the jury in the Emerald Rose Case. And he told himself, "I have a bad habit of making things too complicated. Too abstract."

She guessed what he was thinking. "Robert, I know you know how to talk to juries, but it helps to be reminded. For instance, a smarty-pants lawyer might say, 'Mister Witness, how did you perform, with respect to the operation and control of your motor vehicle?'"

She laughed, just to show she knew it sounded silly. "I guess I can figure out what that sentence means, but if I heard it, I don't know if I'd get it right away, and I'd be several questions behind from then on. A better way to say the same thing is, *'How did you drive your car?'*"

"Of course."

His case was technical. But he realized, I can't let that make me talk in a technical way. Instead, I need to work at keeping it simple and straightforward.

Once again, Maria had told him something valuable. She always surprised him.

* * *

Robert didn't exactly have the "week off." There was the matter of planning for the rest of the trial. And also, Judge Preston had ordered a mid-trial hearing to discuss the length of the presentations by the defendants.

Once the judge had taken the bench and addressed each of the lawyers, she asked Jimmy Coleman to estimate how long his part of the case would take.

"Your honor," replied the familiar grating voice, "we think it will take at least ten weeks."

The judge looked astonished. And also, annoyed. "Why do you believe it's going to take you that long?"

"Well, your honor, for several reasons. First, these are not full days. The court has plenty of business concerning other ongoing cases. We've been able to spend only afternoons some days, because mornings were consumed by hearings in other cases. The court absolutely has to take care of all of its business, and so the court is right to take that time for other matters. But it reduces the time for our case."

"Yes, but you've estimated more time for your case than the plaintiffs took."

"Not really, your honor. About the same."

"But you don't have the same amount to prove. For instance, Mr. Herrick had to call each plaintiff. You don't, and you got to cross-examine each one. Mr. Herrick had to establish facts about which you don't have any disagreement, such as how an oil well works, who was on the platform, and a hundred other items. You don't have to re-do that."

"But Mr. Herrick didn't do anything to prove up our defenses. Such as our defense that this was an unavoidable accident, or an Act of God. And also, Mr. Herrick didn't have to prove our defense that everyone on the platform was a 'borrowed servant' of Emerald Petroleum. That would mean we only owe worker's compensation insurance, and it's going to require a large number of witnesses. And although we'd love it if Mr. Herrick didn't cross-examine those witnesses, we assume that he will, and so will every other lawyer in the case."

Judge Preston just shook her head. Finally, she asked lawyers for Dalliman Services and Momex the same question. "How long?"

"For Dalliman, your honor, also about ten weeks."

"Yes. About the same for Momex."

"Again, why?"

"Well, we vigorously oppose Emerald Petroleum's so-called 'borrowed servant' defense. That would have the practical effect of exempting Emerald from liability and loading more on us. In addition, we have unavoidable accident and Act of God defenses too. But ours are different and require different evidence. It's one thing to say that the pressure was unavoidable, and it's another to say that the failure of the Blowout Preventer under that pressure was unavoidable."

"Mr. Herrick?"

"Your honor, these time estimates are wildly exaggerated. Taken together, the defendants are saying they need about two-thirds of a year. They don't. It's a trial tactic. The defendants want to wear out the jury, confuse the issues, and make it so that the plaintiff's case isn't even a faraway memory."

"All right." Judge Preston had heard enough. "Here's what I'm going to do. I'm going to limit the presentation of Emerald Petroleum to five weeks. Dalliman, two weeks. Momex, two weeks. I'll give you a narrow escape valve. If any of the three defendants can show that they've used their weeks efficiently, but they still need more time, I will grant more."

She shook her head again. "But I strongly advise all defendants to try to fit the time limits I've ordered, and to try seriously."

When they left the courtroom, Tom said, "We'll be lucky if the jury remembers anything of our case after three different defendants fill up five weeks, then two more weeks, then still two more weeks, with wrangling that has nothing to do with the plaintiffs."

"I know. For nine weeks, we've got to watch the jury sit there while we hope they remember what we proved to them. And maybe longer, because you know Jimmy will want five more weeks after that. Jimmy definitely won this hearing."

34

Monday morning. Time to start the case for the defense. And Jimmy got right into it.

"Introduce yourself to the jury, please, and tell them your qualifications."

The witness was an old hand at this, and he turned to the jury and smiled. "My name is Maurice Kelly, and I'm a petroleum engineer. I have a degree in chemistry from Harvard, a master's degree in chemical engineering from M.I.T., and a doctorate in petroleum engineering from CalTech—the California Institute of Technology."

"Please tell us about your experience in the industry, Doctor Kelly."

"I worked as a petroleum engineer for Shell and Exxon for a total of twelve years. After that, I set up Kelly Consultants. We advise oil exploration and production companies, particularly offshore."

"Doctor Kelly, you've studied the blowout and explosion at the Emerald Rose. Please tell the jury your conclusion. Was the accident unavoidable?"

"The blowout and explosion at the Emerald Rose was an unavoidable accident, at least from the point of view of Emerald Petroleum."

"It was an unavoidable accident?"

"Absolutely."

"Doctor Kelly, please tell us why you concluded this."

"It's simple. The pressure encountered by the drill stem at the instant that the well reached depth was unprecedented for the area. It far exceeded anything we've encountered there. Even a very prudent operator, who used equipment and methods greater and safer than usual, would not have been able to contain this pressure. And that's the whole story, right there."

"Do you have a conclusion as to whether the blowout and explosion was an Act of God, as that term is defined at law?"

"Yes, I do. It was an Act of God. Yes, indeed."

"Again, why?"

"An Act of God is similar to an unavoidable accident, but slightly different. It means that the accident normally would not have happened but for the occurrence of an unusual event in nature that could not have been anticipated. Here, the pressure, so far exceeding what would have been expected by any reasonable person, was not capable of being anticipated. And it was an Act of God, as well as an unavoidable accident."

Jimmy questioned the witness for another twenty minutes, mostly going over all the data he had considered and the methods he had used. For an expert witness, it was a short examination. And then, Jimmy said, "No more questions."

It is ridiculous testimony, Robert thought. He said so to Tom during a recess. But he was worried about it.

So was Tom. "The jury isn't like us lawyers. The jury is neutral. Jurors don't usually write off the entire testimony when an expert testifies, even if there's part of it they don't believe. And this guy was straightforward and simple. He spouted some good jury stuff. It's possible he's got the jury considering Jimmy's defenses."

* * *

Cross-examination. Robert's turn with the witness. The recess had ended.

"Good morning, Doctor Kelly. I'm Robert Herrick, and I represent the plaintiffs."

"Yes, I know." The witness smiled. "Good morning, Mr. Herrick."

"Doctor Kelly, I need to ask you about your meeting with Mr. Jimmy Coleman. Of course, he must have told you what kind of testimony he needed, right?"

"Yes, sir."

"And I'm sure, with Mr. Coleman being the defense lawyer, he mentioned the idea of an unavoidable accident?"

"Again, yes, sir."

"And he told you the meaning of this term, unavoidable accident, in the law?"

"Yes, sir."

"And I don't suppose he wrote it down for you. He just defined it himself, using his words, rather than showing you a jury definition in writing, like what this jury is going to get?"

"Well . . . ." Suddenly the witness was wary. "Yes, . . . sir. It was verbal. He told me."

"And he did the same thing in discussing the idea of an Act of God with you, right?"

"I guess. But I don't know what you mean by, 'he did the same thing.'"

Robert was confident that the jurors knew.

"So, it was only after this kind of conversation that Mr. Coleman designated you as an expert witness, isn't that right?"

"Yes, sir."

"And he agreed to pay you four hundred dollars an hour?"

"Yes, sir."

"Now, let me ask you some questions about the Emerald Rose. First, the casing was inadequate, wasn't it?"

"Well, yes. But only because of the unanticipated pressure."

"And it was foolish to replace the drilling mud with sea water, which was guaranteed not to hold the pressure?"

"Maybe. But it was subject to a blowout anyway, even with normal drilling mud."

"Heavy mud could have held it, right?"

The witness shrugged. "Depends on how heavy."

"Now, you've talked about how high the pressure was in this area. But pressure varies from well to well, doesn't it?"

"Absolutely." The witness nodded and smiled. This was an easy answer.

"And whatever we may have been used to in this area, there's been pressure as high as the Emerald Rose had, in other areas of the world?"

"Yes."

"And higher?"

"Yes."

"In fact, there have been wells reaching pressures this high or higher right here in the Gulf of Mexico, right?"

"I suppose so. But not in Keathley Canyon." It was a weak answer.

"It would have been more careful to have kept heavy drilling mud in place and to have had better casing, wouldn't it?"

"I suppose so." The witness hesitated. "But then, no one would have anticipated this pressure in this location, so they wouldn't have known that keeping heavy mud was a good idea."

Robert started to argue with that, but then thought better of it. You usually don't win by arguing conclusions with a witness.

"That's all. Thank you, Doctor Kelly."

* * *

Another recess. The trial resumed with Doctor Kelly still on the witness stand.

"Doctor," Jimmy said, "You prepared raw calculations and also a chart showing your calculations before this trial. Let me show you what have been marked as Emerald Exhibit 45 and Emerald Exhibit 46. Are these Exhibits, 45 and 46, your calculations and your chart?"

"Yes."

"What was the purpose of these calculations?"

"To figure out what would have happened if the casing had been one grade higher and if more of the existing mud had been left in place."

"And, looking at the chart in Exhibit 46, what did your calculations show?"

"Even with those two changes, the pressure at the drill stem would have been too great to hold. There would have been a blowout anyway. And I should add, there was no reason to anticipate this."

Jimmy had been lying in wait with this set of Exhibits. They had been disclosed during discovery, but Jimmy had released them with a mass of other documents and avoided giving away their significance.

Now, he passed the witness.

Robert questioned the calculations during re-cross-examination. "What you're really saying, Doctor, is that the casing was seriously inadequate, so inadequate that upgrading it by one little notch wouldn't have changed the result?" "And the same with the drilling mud, because it was inadequate too, according to you?"

But he left the courtroom with the conviction that Doctor Kelly had succeeded at undermining his case.

Once again, Jimmy had gained the upper hand.

The plaintiffs were losing.

35

"Hi. My name is Gabriel, and I'm an alcoholic."

The man stood in front of perhaps two dozen spectators. Some were visitors. Some were regulars. He wore suit trousers and a white dress shirt from which he had removed his tie. He was clean-shaven, tanned, and healthy- and wealthy-looking.

"Hi, Gabriel," answered the small crowd.

"It's a real surprise to me to be here." Gabriel looked down. "I didn't know the signs. Didn't know I needed to know them. My cousin gave me an AA list of the characteristics that make up an alcoholic. I went over the list, but not very seriously. A month later, I had a wreck. I was drunk. I ruined my car and caused more than ten thousand dollars damage to the other guy's car."

The man hesitated. "I didn't get arrested. But I realized that the only reason was that no one thought to call the police. The other guy looked at me in a funny way, but I acted as sober as I could. All the while, I knew why the wreck had happened. I was drunk."

"Next day, I looked at the list. Asked myself the questions. 'Did I miss work because of drinking?' Yes. 'Did I drink alone?' Yes. 'Did I drink on purpose to get drunk?' Yes. And on and on."

Pepper Herrick sat in the third row. She waffled between denial—"I am not like this broken-down guy, this guy in front of us"—and self-recognition—"Yes, I do all of those things too, and I've even been to jail."

"About the twelve step program," Gabriel went on, "I will start very systematically next week on a step that's hard to do. I'll be locating everyone I've hurt by my drinking and drunkenness. It has to

176

include the guy I had the wreck with, of course. The insurance has settled up, and my insurance premiums have gone through the roof, but I need to gut up and tell that guy, "I was drunk and I'm sorry."

The audience buzzed with whispers about that.

"And the most prominent people I have to apologize to are my wife and my two teenage sons. Why she still hangs around me, I don't know. But I appreciate it. I have a lot of specific things to make up for. And a lot of apologizing to do."

Pepper stayed back, in the last row, for the entire meeting. She was here as an onlooker, a spectator, not as a real participant. But at this point, her eyes were wide, her mouth was open, and her hand was spread across her face.

* * *

The next morning, Jimmy Coleman called his second witness.

"Doctor Melasky," he asked, "did you have occasion to examine a person named Bertrand Bening?"

"Yes." The witness leafed through a report.

"And you've been told that Bertrand Bening is one of the plaintiffs who suffered burns on the Emerald Rose platform. And did you read the testimony that the plaintiffs have offered about this plaintiff?"

"Yes, sir."

"Did you reach any conclusions about the testimony offered by the plaintiffs and the actual condition of Bertrand Bening?"

"Yes, sir. The plaintiffs made it sound as though the picture for Mr. Bening was gloomy. It is true that he suffered second and third degree burns to his face, neck, arms and hands, among other parts of his body. He lost three fingers. But Mr. Bening's remaining injuries are capable of healing completely."

"Can you provide us with more detail about Mr. Bening's prognosis?"

"His arms already have good range of motion. His hands open and close, as if there had been no injury. Perhaps not completely, but nearly as if there had been no injury. His face and neck, with skin grafts and plastic surgery, will be intact."

Jimmy concentrated on Bertrand Bening for twenty more minutes. Then he shifted to another one of the surviving plaintiffs. Then another. Then still another.

This witness, Doctor Melasky, had not seen all of the plaintiffs. But it took three days of testimony for him to go through all of the ones he had examined. He added that later, another doctor would talk about the plaintiffs that he, Doctor Melasky, had not seen.

* * *

Robert Herrick had taken notes throughout Doctor Melasky's testimony. The notes were twelve pages long.

But he deliberately reminded himself about his visit to the art museum with Maria. "You're too scholarly," he reminded himself. "Don't talk to the jury the way an art critic would."

He thought about his lengthy dissertations on Picasso's works. "Don't," he told himself. He thought carefully about Maria's advice. "Simple and straightforward." And again, "Simple and straightforward."

"Good morning, Doctor Melasky."

"Good morning." The doctor was wary. Good.

"What it amounts to, Doctor, is that you think the plaintiffs are faking it. Isn't that right?"

Robert had chosen this beginning because it was simple and straightforward. Also, he chose it because he wanted to get the witness to start denying everything. He wanted Doctor Melasky to disagree with every suggestion he made of serious injuries.

"No," said Doctor Melasky firmly. "Some of what they say isn't faked."

Good. After that answer, the jurors were looking quizzically at Doctor Melasky already.

"Every single one of them is hurt badly. Isn't that true?"

"No." Doctor Melasky looked annoyed. An indefensible answer, thought Robert. Good.

"Take Bertrand Bening. He was the first one you talked about. It's true that he won't recover his full range of arm movement, isn't it?"

"No. That's not true." By now, the Doctor had decided that his job was to contradict whatever Mr. Herrick suggested. "He absolutely can recover his range of motion."

"Well, Doctor, we've also heard testimony that Mr. Bening will never be able to be an oilfield worker again. The only line of work he knows. I suppose you know that Mr. Bening can't ever do that kind of work again."

"I know no such thing! He will be perfectly able to do this work."

"But his having lost three fingers and being unable to close his hands will keep him from doing any kind of oil field work, or construction, or outdoor work, won't it?"

"Certainly not." The doctor was hostile by now. "Handicapped people can do all kinds of things."

Robert stared at the witness. Keep it simple.

And if the witness uses terminology that condemns all of his testimony, the cross-examiner should adopt that testimony too.

"He is, indeed, badly handicapped, Mr. Bening is. Right?"

"Not really handicapped." Suddenly, the witness was trying to retreat. "And not badly."

"He used to enjoy bowling and playing tennis. He can't do those things any more, can he?"

"He can grip harder to hold the racket. If he's strong and determined. Yes, he can play tennis."

Some of the jurors were covering their eyes at this point. And now, Jimmy Coleman asked the judge for a recess. The reason was obvious to everybody, including the jurors. He needed to have a serious talk with his witness.

"That's denied," said Judge Preston. "We'll break at midmorning, as usual."

Robert continued the cross-examination. He used the word "handicapped" in his questions to the doctor about each injured plaintiff. The word the witness had used.

During the midmorning recess, Jimmy had had a chance to "woodshed" the witness, as a lawyer would say. His testimony changed. He was a little more willing to agree that the plaintiffs were hurt. He just pushed back at the idea that they were "badly" hurt.

* * *

Jimmy was waiting his turn. The picture looked grim for him, at least with this witness. But Robert knew that Jimmy would have something up his sleeve during redirect examination.

And he knew that Jimmy knew how to keep it simple and straightforward too—while attacking Robert's case.

"Doctor Melasky," Jimmy began, "are you, yourself, a burn victim too?"

"Yes, sir." The doctor looked subdued.

"How did it happen?"

"An accident with a water heater. You should never store flammable chemicals nearby."

"Your burn scars are where, Doctor?"

"My chest, legs, arms, and hands are scarred. My neck and face were too, but grafts and surgery were able to minimize those." The doctor held up his hands so that the scars were visible.

"Did you have complete range of motion right after your accident, or right after your early treatment, Doctor?"

"No. But fortunately, nobody told me to feel limited. Nobody told me I couldn't do anything. I know now that I was lucky. These plaintiffs have been taught that they are handicapped, and that is very unlucky for them."

The doctor looked at Robert Herrick as if to say, you've hurt your own clients, because you've told them to be helpless.

"Doctor, does it depend on the attitude of the patient, as to how much range of motion can be recovered?"

"It sure does."

"Doctor, does it also depend on the patient's willingness to work on doing exercises, take on tasks, and take on activities that they used to like?"

"It sure does."

Robert stared at the witness. And he stared at Jimmy. He knew that he had seriously wounded this doctor in cross-examination. But Jimmy was well on his way toward saving the witness and, maybe, making him even more credible than he would have been without the cross-examination.

Once again, Robert saw that the jury had every reason to favor the defense.

36

That evening, Robert turned his car into the parking lot beside the green-and-orange sign that said, "Sunrise Green. . . . This is your home." Regardless of trouble with his case, losing or not, he intended to visit his mother as scheduled.

"Hi, Mom. I mean, hi, Rosalie."

She smiled. "Hi, little Robert. I'm so glad you're here."

"Me too."

"I've been thinking about Pepper. Remind me. Pepper is your cousin?"

"My daughter. Your granddaughter."

"So, what's happening with Pepper?" By now, Rosalie Herrick was much less embarrassed by her forgetfulness than she once had been. She was just as likely, still, not to remember. She just avoided being bothered by it.

"Pepper has serious problems with alcohol. She can't stop getting drunk. It's a terrible thing. At times, I think we're going to lose her."

"I understand. What can be done?"

"Right now, we're trying to get her to go to AA. Alcoholics Anonymous. She's gone to a meeting and looked at it, but she's dead set against it. She says she isn't an alcoholic and doesn't want to lie about being one."

"How would that be lying?"

"It wouldn't. It's just an excuse. But she has a lot of excuses. Most of them are about her claiming that she is not anything like those . . . *losers* at AA, as she puts it."

"And you want her to go. And stand up and say, 'I'm an alcoholic.'"

"Yes. Because that's what she is. She's an alcoholic."

"Well, little Robert. It's a conundrum. I always like to say, It's a conundrum. Because I like that word. Conundrum. So, anyway, I know what you can say to your daughter. What's her name? Pepper?"

He listened.

"You didn't ever know it, Robert, but my Frederick drank too much. You never knew, but there was a time when he drank way too much. He got drunk. Frequently. I think he was an alcoholic, although we were less likely to say that back then. One time, I got rid of all the bourbon in the house. He solved that problem by breaking into the liquor store."

"He did *what?*"

"He broke into the liquor store. He knew the store, and he got in through the back. He stole a couple of bottles of bourbon. The alarm went off, and he ran, and he got away with it. I got really mad and went to my mother's house. I took you with me, little Robert. You never knew."

"Good grief."

"That was your daddy. Your daddy, who was so capable. And so dignified. And it got handed down to Pepper, you know. You should tell her. He got the message after that, thank goodness. And he straightened up, just by deciding to do it. Some people can do that and some people can't."

"All . . . right. . . . So, I should tell her. . . ."

"Yes. And Robert, you yourself have that love for too much alcohol in you, too. From time to time, you drink too much. Much, much too much. You use it as a crutch. That's the same thing Pepper does."

He looked at the floor.

"Tell her about my Frederick, her grandfather. And tell her about you. And tell her that Grandma Rosalie insists that she go to AA." Her voice rose. "She's got to go!"

While he drove home, Robert wondered about people with Alzheimer's Disease. They suffer a terrifying loss of memory. A scary kind of forgetfulness. But then, he thought, they replace it with an episodic, wandering wisdom on unpredictable subjects. An uncommon, floating awareness of what to do in difficult situations. And sometimes, major memories.

He would talk to Pepper, armed with this information from Rosalie Herrick.

And he could hope that she would listen.

* * *

The next witnesses Jimmy called to the stand were Emerald Petroleum employees. And Jimmy made it clear why they were called. Their testimony was designed to prove that every individual on the platform was really an Emerald employee, a "borrowed servant," no matter who wrote his paycheck.

"We're gonna show that everybody was a borrowed servant," bragged one of the black-suited associates who had an unusually big mouth. "Then, Robert Herrick, Emerald's not liable for anything in this lawsuit. All you get is worker's compensation insurance."

Which is a small fraction of their real damages in this lawsuit, Robert thought unhappily.

"State your name for the members of the jury, please," Jimmy began.

"Alphonse Hebert, pronounced Ay-bear," the witness answered. "I was one of de t'ree tool pushas on de platfoam."

"We've seen you once before, Mr. AY-bear?"

"Correct. I was de one who opposed putting sea water in place a de drillin mud. Mr. Herrrick called me to de witness stand to testify about dat."

"So, I guess Mr. Herrick thought you were credible."

"Objection, your honor." Robert was on his feet in an instant.

"Sustained," said the judge. "The jury will ignore that last remark of counsel and consider it for no purpose."

But Jimmy and the witness just smiled. They had made their point.

"When you were on duty, Mr. AY-bear, did you have power over every employee, to tell them what to do?"

"Ab-so-lutely."

"And did every employee follow your directions?"

"Dey knew dey bettah follow dem. You know, not ev'abody do what dey supposed to all de time, but if dey didn't do what I said, dey got in trouble."

"Are you familiar with what a 'borrowed servant' is, in the law?"

"Yes sah."

"Was every employee on the Emerald Rose platform a borrowed servant of Emerald, whom you had the power to command?"

"Yes sah."

It was all simple and straightforward.

And Jimmy passed the witness.

Robert was ready to cross-examine. "Mr. AY-bear, when the stewards made the beds in the habitation, did they use fitted sheets, or did they make hospital corners?"

"Huh? What?"

"That's what I thought. You didn't supervise the stewards in making the beds, did you? Or even know what they did?"

"No."

"You didn't oversee how the cooks cooked, or how the stevedores loaded up deliveries of pipe or anything else, or how the firefighters did their jobs?"

"No."

"Now, I take it that what you're really saying is that if any of these people strayed into the drilling area, you had charge of that area?"

"Ab-so-lutely. Ev'abody bettah listen to me, den."

"So, it's kind of like, if I go into the police station, I have to do what the police tell me, while I'm in the police station. That's how people better pay attention to you in the drilling area?"

"Ab-so-lutely."

"But that doesn't mean that if I go into the police station, I immediately become an employee of the police department, does it?"

The witness scatched his chin. "No. It's not de same t'ing."

"And if I just happen to go into the police station, that doesn't magically make me some kind of 'borrowed servant' of the police?"

"Not de same t'ing."

Robert was ready to pass the witness, but he whispered with Tom Kennedy. Then, he sat up straight.

"Mr. AY-bear, as Mr. Coleman implied, you had credibility when you told us it was negligent to replace the drilling mud with sea water. But as your answers to these questions show, you don't have any credibility about who's a borrowed servant, do you?"

Jimmy stood up immediately. "I object. That's a highly improper question."

The jurors started laughing. So did the judge, in spite of herself. "That's sustained."

Robert had scored.

* * *

Jimmy Coleman was unfazed. He called four more witnesses to support his "borrowed servant" defense. The testimony lasted for days.

What's more, Jimmy lined up a dozen additional witnesses to testify to the same thing.

At this point, while the jury was in the jury room, Robert stood. "Judge, I object. The testimony is cumulative. In fact, this is the ideal example of what we as lawyers call cumulative testimony."

"That's sustained. Mr. Coleman, each of these five witnesses has said the same thing. There's nothing new, as I understand it. Please inform me if any of this mass of witnesses is going to talk about something really new. Otherwise, the testimony is excluded."

"Yes, your honor." Jimmy smiled, and so did his entourage of black-suited associates, to let the judge know that they were untroubled by her ruling.

37

The defense case droned on. For weeks.

Jimmy had more physician witnesses. More engineering witnesses. Geophysical witnesses. Safety witnesses. A labor economist, to disagree with the plaintiffs' labor economist. A rehabilitation witness. Witnesses who had been present on the platform. And every one of them considered something in the testimony that Robert's witnesses had offered, and every one told the jurors why Robert's witness was absolutely, definitely wrong.

In Robert's mind, the defense witnesses threatened to become a blur, in which nothing really mattered. He reminded himself that a trial rewards lawyers with stamina. The ability to stay with the battle, when others tire, is more important, even, than eloquence.

"The jury's eyes are glazing over, the same way ours are," Tom Kennedy reassured him. "Jimmy has overdone it. As Shakespeare said, *'To gild refined gold, to paint the lily, is wasteful and ridiculous excess.'* That's what Jimmy's doing. And he's losing the jury."

The unorthodox appeal to Shakespeare, with this unnecessary but apt rhetorical flourish, drew a laugh from Robert, tired as he was.

With this mindset, he went on to cross-examine each witness. But he agreed with Tom, and he kept his questioning as short as he could. Sometimes, jurors can sniff out a lawyer who is dragging out a trial, and they punish him by deciding that he's doing it because he doesn't have a good case.

The defense slouched into its fifth week. And on the last day of that week, presumably because of Judge Preston's order, Jimmy stood up and said, "The defendant, Emerald Petroleum, rests."

* * *

When lawyers for Dalliman Services started to present their case, the jury visibly showed signs of weariness with the whole thing.

But Dalliman had to have a chance to defend itself, separately. Its witnesses talked first about the Blowout Preventer. That device would have worked fine if it had not been up against pressure that Emerald should have known would overcome it. And that wouldn't have happened if Emerald had paid attention to the gas bubbling into the drill stem, if it had kept heavy mud in place instead of light sea water, and if it had not had inadequate casing.

Finally, there was testimony offered by Momex. This corporation had supplied and monitored diagnostic equipment: the electronics that measured the pressure. Its witnesses pointed out that Momex had notified Emerald of conditions on a continuous basis.

* * *

It was in the middle of Momex's testimony that Robert thought he finally had persuaded Pepper. But then, he realized that he hadn't.

"So my grandfather was an alcoholic. And you, my daddy—you've gone through periods when you drank too much. How does it affect me?"

"Pepper, please. This isn't nice for me either. And the answer is, yes, it affects you."

"How? I'm an individual. I'm as different from both of you as I am from those pathetic people who show up at the AA meetings. For one thing, I'm female. My entire physiology is different."

"Pepper, again, please. The answer is that alcohol abuse runs in families. I passed on good things to you, and I made sure you had every opportunity. But I am realizing, now, that I passed on something bad too."

"But I don't think so. How do you claim it gets passed on?"

"First of all, by attitudes toward alcohol. A family like ours, from what I understand, is particularly likely to pass it on. High expectations on the kids, pressure on the parents, and a daddy and grandfather who tried to solve problems by drinking. Which is not a good example."

"You think that's enough to make me into an alcoholic? An *alco-holic?*"

"Yes. People who have studied it a lot more than I have are unanimous in saying so. And Pepper, if that's not enough, they think that there is a physical predisposition to it, based on genetics. And then, take into account your own difficulties created by alcohol, because that should show you something."

"But Daddy, they're not so much 'difficulties.' The troubles I've had were short-time things. They were blips on the curve. I'm going to drink less, but I'm going to do it myself."

He talked to her many times, allowing periods in between. The conversations always went around in circles.

* * *

After all of the defendants had rested, Robert called one rebuttal witnesses. He was determined to call only one. He was determined to keep it simple. And straightforward.

"Please state your name for the members of the jury."

"John Errol Tull."

"You have testified once before in this case."

"Yes, sir. I was the first witness before the jury. I studied petroleum engineering and gave the jury an outline of how the blowout at the Emerald Rose happened."

"Mr. Tull, we've now completed testimony from both sides. We've heard from the defendants. Witnesses for Emerald Petroleum have testified that the accident happened because the Blowout Preventer didn't prevent it. Witnesses for Dalliman say that it's Emerald's fault because of the sea water, the bubbling gas, and the inadequate casing. Incidentally, does this conflict between the defendants surprise you?"

"No. I expected they'd be pointing fingers at each other."

Jimmy Coleman looked as though he wanted to object, but he didn't. It wouldn't have done any good to get an objection sustained.

"Mr. Tull, do you have an opinion as to which of those two finger-pointers is right?"

"I do."

"And what is that opinion?"

"They're both right. Emerald was extremely careless in all the ways you mentioned. And Dalliman was extremely careless too.

Robert passed the witness.

There wasn't really much that Jimmy Coleman could say, but he tried.

"Mr. Tull, if the Blowout Preventer had worked, we wouldn't be here, would we?"

"No. But you can say the same thing about the sea water, the bubbling gas, and the casing."

"And from Emerald's standpoint, this tragedy was an unavoidable accident. An Act of God. You haven't expressed an opinion on that, have you?"

"No. It sounds like mumbo jumbo to me."

The jurors laughed.

"You must mean you don't understand the possibility of an unavoidable accident. But the law allows for it. If Emerald didn't expect it, it couldn't have prevented it, could it?"

"I suppose not. But shouldn't it have prevented it?"

Jimmy passed the witness. This was as much as he was going to be able to do to John Errol Tull's testimony by cross-examination.

* * *

"This is Charro. Calling from Tamaulipas. I work for El Raton. You know, the man whose complete name is Enrico Pedro Nunez Rodriguez y Cavazos. But you know him as El Raton."

"Yes," said the man at the other end of the line.

"You know how much we want this *gusano*—this worm, this maggot, who is named Tom Kennedy—taken out. Killed. Dead. However you want to say it. Curtains—that's what we want for him. Checkout time. The big sleep. Extinction. Kicking the bucket. Am I spelling it out well enough?"

"Yes. You and I have a contract about that. I am looking for the opportunity."

"But nothing has happened."

"He has never been in a place where I could take him out. Not yet. Be patient, please. What you want will be done."

"El Raton is not patient. He is not happy. And you certainly don't want to have El Raton thinking about you when he is not happy."

"That is more than the truth." The man's voice quavered. "But what can I do? What can I do, if the *gusano* is never where I can do it?"

"That, mi amigo, is your problem. You contracted to do a job. We paid you half and will be happy to pay you the other half when you deliver. It's a lot of money for a little job. But you've got to get it done."

"Does El Raton not understand that this cannot be done when the man is not where it can be done?"

"No. El Raton does not understand excuses. Instead, he understands results."

"But. . . ."

"Mi amigo, you know where he is. Top floor of Texas Commerce Tower. You need to get it done."

38

The charge will be plain vanilla," said the court. "No unusual instructions for the jury. Isn't that right?"

"Yes, your honor," said Robert Herrick. "Except that we don't think that Momex should be listed as a responsible party. That would reduce Emerald's liability, and there's no evidence, in the end, that Momex was negligent at all."

"We disagree," said Jimmy Coleman. "There's plenty of evidence of Momex's negligence."

"Also," said a lawyer for Dalliman, "there's that Act of God defense, which should be submitted to the jury."

"But that's not a separate defense from the unavoidable accident defense," protested the judge.

"Judge, yes, it's a separate defense. We have briefing for you that shows that it is a separate defense. The cases are clear. The jury has to be asked separately about Act of God."

"We agree," grated Jimmy.

"Do you claim that this Act of God defense is an actual question to the jury, or only an instruction saying not to find causal negligence if they find it was an Act of God?"

"Both," said the Dalliman lawyer.

"We agree," grated Jimmy.

"No," said Robert. "Act of God is not a real defense. It just goes into figuring negligence, if it exists, and it doesn't here. We will supply your honor with the cases in our brief."

"Well," said the judge doubtfully, "except for having to resolve these disagreements, the charge and jury instructions will be plain vanilla, won't they?"

"There also is a separate question about who was a borrowed servant, of course." Jimmy sounded adamant about this.

"We disagree," said Robert firmly, "because the evidence is insufficient to even let the jury decide that anyone was a borrowed servant."

"We agree with that," said the Dalliman and Momex lawyers, in chorus. "Emerald shouldn't get away with trying to stick us with damages by claiming that our employees were Emerald's, and covered by Emerald's worker's compensation insurance, when they weren't Emerald's employees at all."

"And your honor," Robert said quickly, "the instructions on negligence should treat the actions of professional individuals such as engineers, whether employed by Emerald, Dalliman, or Momex, as professionals. Just like a physician or an architect. They should exercise the knowledge and skill of professional engineers, and that's what the jury should be told."

The judge was getting unhappier and unhappier.

"Well, judge, we've prepared a complete charge and set of jury instructions for your honor to use," said Jimmy. His voice was like a hacksaw scraping a rusty iron pipe. "Our completed charge will make it easy for you."

"But that charge is offered on behalf of the defendant Emerald, and it's biased." Robert spoke quickly. "In fact, it's erroneous. The plaintiffs have submitted a different charge, and we have made ours conform to the law, not to a defendant's wish list."

"All right. All right!" The judge had heard enough. "I will study all of your proposed charges to the jury. And I will take everything you've said here into account."

It took two days, finally, to hammer out the jury charge and instructions. After the judge had settled on a general shape for the long flow of words that seemed necessary, the attorneys fought over the placement of every comma. They offered proposed synonyms for dozens of words, tried to invert sentences, and spent more than an hour dictating objections into the record.

The next day, the judge would read the charge to the jury. Because there were so many plaintiffs, it was well over a hundred pages long.

And then, the lawyers would give their final arguments to the jury. Which would involve both Robert and Francel.

* * *

Francel Williams stood in front of the jury box at last, ready to give the plaintiffs' opening argument to the jury.

It had taken the judge almost two hours to read the charge and instructions to the jurors out loud. Now, Francel would give the first argument—the plaintiffs' opening argument. Next would be Jimmy Coleman on behalf of Emerald. Then arguments for Dalliman and Momex. And at the end, Robert Herrick would give the plaintiffs' rebuttal argument, or closing argument.

This way, both Francel and Robert would appear before the jury. They had agreed to split the argument. It would take more than two days for the whole process.

"Ladies and gentlemen of the jury," Francel said slowly, with a smile. He was about to begin with a very conventional, tried and true opening line.

". . . I appreciate your service. The plaintiffs all appreciate your service. We have seen that you are an intelligent, hardworking jury. A jury that pays attention to everything. One of our greatest achievements in America is the jury system, and you fine citizens have performed the duty extraordinarily well."

Robert recognized the tactic. The psychologists describe it as the "audience reward" effect. We like people who praise us. We like people who like us back. Robert saw that Francel was tapping into that phenomenon.

But won't the jurors think the lawyer is just buttering them up, to win the case? Won't they think it's insincere? Psychologists say no, and they have experiments to back them up. People normally attribute the actions of others to real sentiments. They attribute praise to sincere feelings. Even when they shouldn't.

And Robert recognized this side of the tactic. Psychologists call it "the fundamental attribution error," and Francel was tapping into this, too, by praising the jurors. And yes, Robert knew, Francel would have done it even in front of jurors who didn't seem so intelligent. Or for that matter, even jurors who had repeatedly fallen asleep.

"So, Ladies and gentlemen, you are a smart group of people." Francel wore a big smile. "You will easily understand the definitions the judge gives you. For example, the judge defines the word 'negligence' in terms of defendants who do what is not reasonable, and who don't exercise proper care. In ordinary language, negligence means *carelessness*. Which is exactly what Mr. Herrick told you at the beginning of this trial. *Carelessness*."

The instructions actually define negligence with a long list of more complicated words. But this, too, was a standard tactic. A pole vaulter trying to clear a high bar can get a longer pole—or he can lower the bar. Robert knew that this resembles what a trial lawyer does. You can get evidence that's as powerful as possible, and that's like the pole vaulter getting a longer pole, or you can lower the bar, by proposing a meaning of negligence that's easier to overcome. Negligence sounds hard to prove. "Carelessness" sounds easier.

"The first question, ladies and gentlemen, is 'Whose negligence, if anyone's, was a proximate cause of the occurrence at issue in this case?' And that means, simply, 'Who was careless in causing this disaster that killed so many people?'"

Francel pointed at the court's jury instructions. "The possible answers that the judge gives you are Emerald Petroleum Company, Dalliman Services, and Momex Offshore.

"The answer is, Emerald was negligent, and so was Dalliman."

Francel's argument took a half day's worth of courtroom time. He repeated for the jury all of the evidence that supported these findings of negligence. And he went through all of the plaintiffs and pointed out the damages and losses for each one.

But what he didn't do was to get emotional. He avoided expressing emotion and was simple and logical. Emotion has its place, he and Robert both thought to themselves. But the plaintiffs would have another opportunity to talk to the jury, *after* all of the defendants had finished their arguments. That was the time for pounding the table. If Francel did it now, he would give the defendants the opportunity to criticize him for it. If Robert did it at the end, it would be beyond their ability to ridicule.

Finally, Francel finished showing how the evidence made each defendant liable. He had refuted each of their defenses and pointed to the testimony that proved every plaintiff's damages, He made a short, unemotional closing.

"That's the plaintiffs' case, ladies and gentlemen. The defendants were horribly careless. They killed a large number of people, and they hurt all of the plaintiffs badly. The evidence proves it. In fact, the evidence more than carries the plaintiffs' burden of proof. They are asking for a verdict that is consistent with the evidence. They are begging you for a verdict that is consistent with the evidence. Thank you."

* * *

"I too want to thank you, members of the jury." Jimmy Coleman's voice grated as usual, but he put as much sunshine into it as anyone could. "You are a very smart jury, and I know you will be able to see past what the plaintiffs have argued.

"Francel Williams bent the truth over and over again, just now. For example, he claimed damages that far exceed reality. Did you notice, he didn't mention the doctors that we, Emerald Petroleum, brought to you? One of our doctors was a burn victim himself, and he told you that the plaintiffs' lawyers are hurting their own clients by encouraging them to be dependent."

Jimmy shook his head. "But the plaintiffs' argument is a scatter-shot. It's a blunderbuss argument. It's impossible, unless I talked for a week, to answer everything Mr. Williams has said that's wrong. In-stead, I trust you to weed out the errors. And now, I want to talk to you about what this case is really about."

The defense lawyer held the judge's instructions up. "The judge doesn't tell you that negligence is carelessness. Mr. Williams said it wrong. The judge tells you that negligence means doing something that a reasonable person would not do, or not doing what a reasonable person would do. In other words, Mr. Williams has misrepresented what negligence is. What the judge tells you is that you can't find someone to be negligent unless they are *guilty* of an *unreasonable* act."

Jimmy was nearly shouting as he said it. "And these aren't my words. These are the judge's words, telling you the law. Mr. Williams has distorted those words."

The chubby defense lawyer waved the court's instructions and stabbed his finger at them. "And if we look to the correct law, when the judge asks whether Emerald was negligent and caused this accident, the answer is a resounding *No*.

"The witnesses said that this was an unprecedented amount of pressure. Emerald had no reason to anticipate it. Nobody would have anticipated it. Emerald used careful, prudent methods. And the pressure would have caused the blowout even with heavier drilling mud and even with a bigger casing! In fact, if you think about it, those actions probably would have caused even more pressure to build up. And a bigger blowout."

Now, Jimmy pointed to another part of the instructions. "The judge tells you that there are happenings that we call 'unavoidable accidents.' Here it is, on page four. 'An event may be an unavoidable accident, that is, an event not caused by the negligence of any person.' And that's what this was. An unavoidable accident."

Jimmy talked about his other defenses. Every person on the platform was managed by Emerald, and they were all Emerald employees. "See the definition of a 'borrowed servant' on page thirteen. It fits everyone."

He took pains to cover all of the questions in the charge about damages. And he closed by ridiculing the death claims. "Imagine! What if everyone—everyone who had a relative who died—everyone really ran away with the millions that these lawyers want? All of them could invest those huge, princely sums in municipal bonds, and they would live the rest of their lives high on the hog. All tax-free."

Jimmy's face was twisted into a mask of disgust. "These people are trying to get rich by exploiting a disaster and trading on the bodies of the dead."

It was Jimmy at his best. The jurors were with him. Robert could see it in their faces.

39

L adies and gentlemen of the jury." Robert Herrick stood ramrod straight, looking into their eyes, ready to give the last closing argument. "In just a few short moments, we will entrust this case to you. You've been an excellent jury and we know you will work hard at it."

He lifted a hand to signal a new subject. "I disagree with a lot of what Jimmy Coleman said. I have no quarrel with Mr. Coleman, person to person. He's just doing his job. We knew even before we heard any evidence that he would be arguing that Emerald wasn't negligent, because that's his job."

Robert pointed to the third page of the jury instructions. "Mr. Coleman told you that negligence isn't carelessness. But here are the judge's words. Negligence means acting without what the judge calls 'ordinary care,' the care that a reasonable person would exercise. That's carelessness, no matter how Mr. Coleman slices it. And these are the judge's words, not mine."

He pointed to another page. "And I disagree with how Mr. Coleman claims that everybody on the platform was Emerald Petroleum's employee. In the first place, that's his effort to zero out Emerald's own negligence, so Emerald would owe only piddling amounts of worker's compensation insurance. In the second place, the evidence doesn't fit it at all. Here's what the judge says about borrowed servants. They'd have to be directed by Emerald. But the people on the platform were supervised, directed, and paid by Dalliman, Momex, and Amadanko.

"Now," he said firmly," I want to talk to you about what this case is really about.

"The first question the judge asks you is, 'Whose negligence was a proximate cause' of this disaster?

"Remember, that question just means, 'who was careless?' And the answer is, both Emerald and Dalliman were careless."

He held up one finger. "First, Emerald dumped in sea water to save money. Negligence. Emerald ignored gas bubbling into the drill stem. Negligence. Emerald used casing that was inadequate—and couldn't hold the pressure. Negligence. And Emerald deliberately created an anti-safety culture. Negligence."

A second finger. "Then, there's Dalliman. What did Dalliman do? Used a Blowout Preventer that was inadequate to the task. Negligence. And Dalliman failed to monitor the Blowout Preventer, even when there was gas bubbling into the well, signaling that a blowout was coming. Negligence."

Robert put his hands down and stepped to the other end of the jury rail. "The judge's second question asks, What percentage of the negligence is each of these parties responsible for? And the answer I suggest is, fifty percent to Emerald and fifty percent to Dalliman.

"These percentages are based on the evidence. The Emerald Rose Disaster would not have happened unless Emerald Petroleum was negligent. It also would not have happened unless Dalliman was negligent. They both acted at the same time, with about the same degree of carelessness. That's why I say fifty-fifty."

He held up a chart, and he pointed to the same chart on the projector screen. "The rest of the questions are about the damages to each plaintiff. There are more than a hundred questions. This chart, which is part of the evidence as Plaintiff's Exhibit 115, shows the damages to each plaintiff that we have proved. You can take it back to the jury room.

"It adds up to more than eight hundred million dollars. That may sound like a huge sum. It's not. It's a much smaller amount for each person killed or injured. How much is a human life worth, after all?"

Now, Robert held up a fistful of exhibits. "It's time, ladies and gentlemen of the jury, for the most painful part of the trial. It's time for the Roll Call of the Dead."

He set a photograph on an easel. "This is Sanford Westhoven. Randy Westhoven's beloved Daddy, shown here during his lifetime." Next, he replaced the photograph with another image—one that showed what looked like a lump of coal in the shape of a human face. "This too is Sanford Westhoven, after the defendants' negligence burned him to death."

The jurors gasped, even though they had seen these pictures before. It was the combination of the two photographs that struck them so hard.

"Next on the Roll Call of the Dead is Lucien Boudreaux." And Robert again showed a lifetime photograph, then replaced it with a thoroughly burned image.

At the end, it was time to call on the jury for help. To ask them to carry out the law.

There is a moment in a trial when the plaintiff can do this, can ask the jury for help. Do it too early, and it sounds hollow. Do it too late, and you've missed the opportunity.

"Now it is up to you, ladies and gentlemen. I can do my job and present all of the evidence. The judge can do her job and keep this trial on track. The witnesses can do their job and tell you what happened, and be cross-examined by someone like Mr. Coleman, with all the pain it causes. Even the legislature can do its job—yes, sometimes even the legislature does a good job—by passing laws about negligence.

"But now, we need your help. I need your help. The plaintiffs need your help.

"Because none of it matters without you. You are the last, most important link in the law. I ask you—in fact, I *beg* you—for a verdict that says that the defendants did exactly what they did, and that awards the plaintiffs the damages that the evidence cries out for."

* * *

It was an hour after the jurors had shuffled toward the jury room when Robert and Tom stood up from counsel table and walked toward the courtroom exit.

Robert had gone over it all in his mind. Sometimes silently, sometimes talking to Tom. Jimmy Coleman's argument had been tight and logical in the places where it should have been, and yet it had thundered with powerful emotion where it should have. Robert's own words to the jury, he thought, were uncertain. Meandering. Not completely coherent.

He pictured the jury returning a verdict finding none of the defendants negligent. A zero verdict for the plaintiffs. Jimmy's argument had made a persuasive case for that.

He foresaw it. The plaintiffs were going to lose. And lose big.

Alternatively, he saw a verdict sheet that found the defendants liable. But then the verdict said that all of the employees on the platform were borrowed servants. Emerald Petroleum employees. And it also said that Emerald was the party that was responsible for ninety percent of the negligence. Then, Emerald would owe nothing other than tiny amounts of worker's compensation insurance, and only ten percent of the damages would be payable by Dalliman.

And another possibility was that the jurors could find the defendants liable but slash the damages to a tiny fraction. They would do this if they agreed with Jimmy's argument that the plaintiffs' claims were grossly inflated.

There were so many ways for the plaintiffs to lose.

He saw that he had a telephone call coming in. Quickly, he switched on his phone.

The call was from Maria.

"It's Pepper." Maria Melendes's voice was sad. "Again."

He froze. Had Pepper gotten arrested, now, for driving while intoxicated? Again? Or worse, had she drunkenly caused a wreck and killed someone this time?

"She's in Methodist Hospital," said Maria "In one of the ICU's. An Intensive Care Unit. With acute alcohol poisoning."

He was speechless. "What . . . ahhh . . . what . . . ahhh. . . ."

"I'm on the way over there," Maria spoke quickly. "I don't suppose I'll be able to see her right away, but I'll be there at whatever time they'll let me."

He heard himself saying, "I'm on the way there too."

There are times when events take over and human beings are reduced to something like puppets. Robert wasn't quite aware of what he was hearing from Maria. Or of what he was saying back to her. The whole thing felt as though he were watching himself in a movie. He was completely out of control over what he saw, or heard, or did.

* * *

She was asleep, lying on her back, with her mouth open. At least she was breathing. She had a forest of tubes around her, including one that disappeared into her nose. Visiting time was from five in the afternoon until six, and they had waited three hours to see her. Jonathan, Pepper's husband, had joined them. Now, the three of them stood beside her.

But they hesitated even to say anything.

"It happens," said the volunteer who had brought them back to her bed. "You come to her, and she's asleep. Talk to her. If she doesn't respond, she probably needs to sleep."

"Thank you," said Robert, and the volunteer turned to go.

The ICU wasn't private at all. One bed was lined up next to another. They were six deep on one side, with two at the end, and six more on the other side. The walls were an indeterminate beige, and there were no windows. It seemed strange, because Methodist, like other hospitals, had discovered the benefit of cheery surroundings, at least in the rest of the building. Robert wondered why the ICU, where cheerfulness would seem to matter most, was so depressing. Maybe it had something to do with maintaining sterile conditions? . . . Probably not.

Nurses in uniforms of various colors worked constantly. He noticed that doctors were deferential to the ICU nurses. Odd, because he was used to seeing doctors talk down to nurses. These nurses were too valuable for that. The bustling nurses contrasted to overly casually dressed visitors, who either waited helplessly, the way that Robert and Maria and Jonathan were waiting, or tried to make conversation in a place where there were no natural subjects of conversation.

"Pepper," said Maria softly. Then a little louder: "Pepper."

The sleeping girl stirred but didn't open her eyes.

Jonathan spoke up. "Pepper . . . . Pepper."

One eye opened, fluttering. Then the other, also fluttering.

"We're here. We love you, Pepper. We love you."

She looked but didn't say anything.

Then she turned slightly and said one word. "Sorry."

"Don't worry about being sorry, my beautiful daughter." Robert said it gently but firmly. "We understand that you will be all right. That's what matters."

"Yes," said Jonathan. "That's what matters."

"I'm sorry." She could speak with the tube in her nose, but in a mushy way.

"Don't worry about being sorry."

There was a long pause.

Then, "I've learned my lesson from this." Pepper blinked and blinked again. "I have. I've really learned my lesson."

"Well, that's good. We just want you home now. Or as soon as possible."

"I've learned my lesson."

They waited. Hopeful. Is she going to say she's going to Alcoholics Anonymous? We can hope. . . .

"This was not a good idea. I will have to manage it better. I can do that."

"How?"

"I've overcome other things in my life. Will power. I can keep from overdoing it. I just won't drink as much. I've learned my lesson."

Robert and Maria looked at each other. They could still hope, maybe. But Pepper didn't sound very much like a new member planning to join AA.

40

The jury was out for two days. But that wasn't surprising, since there were more than a hundred questions to answer.

Then they were out for three days. Four days. Five.

And then, they were into their second week.

In his big corner office, Jimmy Coleman met with Jennifer Lowenstein, both of them sitting beside his priceless Italian chest. Jimmy was wearing a big smile. A growing smile that Jennifer had been watching for several days now.

"Why are they out for so long, Jimmy?"

"There is a conflict between what their hearts want and what their heads tell them. That's usually the reason."

"Okay. What do their heads and hearts want?"

"Simple. They see that the plaintiffs' losses are real. They would like to help the plaintiffs. But their heads are telling them that the correct answers to the questions will mean that the defendants will win. That we, on behalf of Emerald Petroleum, will win."

"And what does the conflict mean?"

"If it goes on this long, it's hard to tell. But I think it's good news for Emerald Petroleum. If the plaintiffs are ahead, it's usually easy for the jurors to find ways to say that the plaintiffs win. The longer it takes, the clearer it is that the jurors think the real winners, aside from emotion, are the defendants."

"Do you think the jury is divided into different groups?"

"Probably. The usual lineup in this kind of situation involves a group that favors the plaintiffs and a group that favors the defense. And usually, the plaintiffs' group is the bigger group. That's the people-pleasing jurors. But the pro-defendant group is better at arguing and also is much more tenacious. Ordinarily, when the plaintiffs' group finally gets tired, the defendant group can persuade a couple of those jurors. And sooner or later, the dam breaks and the jurors come over to the defense side."

"That's what you think is probably happening?"

"Not necessarily. It's hard to predict. You can know what happens most of the time. But you can't know what's happening in this case."

"It's an unusual case."

"Yes, it is. It's a case with clear losses by the plaintiffs and a terrible disaster that theoretically could have been prevented."

"Well, but Jimmy, you seem upbeat. Happy about the situation. And yet we don't know. Why are you pleased by this delay?"

"It's a real victory to have the jury out this long and to have a major shot at winning. Remember, the defendants are all pointing fingers at each other. That makes it hard for the defendants to win. But now, I think we have a better chance than the plaintiffs. I think we have a good chance to win."

* * *

Across town, Tom Kennedy sat across the desk from Robert Herrick. They took turns looking out the floor-to-ceiling windows at the point where the green of Buffalo Bayou and Memorial Park faded into the horizon. And they alternated at looking down at the magnificent, multicolored carpet upon which they were sitting.

"What do you think, Tom?"

"I'd say that every day the jury is out makes the odds worse for us."

"Me too, I'm sad to say."

"It's hard to concentrate on anything else."

"It is, yes. But we'd better. We need to figure out which of these new cases to accept, out of the cases that have been referred to us."

"Sometimes I wish we could just tell all the lawyers who refer cases to us to stop for a little while so we can catch our breath."

"But if we do that, we won't have anything to do six months from now. Or a year from now."

"Well, I wonder about this case here." Tom held up a file. "Guy named Pryzyby goes in for a kidney operation. There's a sponge left inside. The scrub nurse doesn't do the sponge count right and the result is that they sew up old Prysyby with the sponge inside. He has a big, bad infection and they have to go back inside to get the sponge out."

"You sound like you like this case, Tom."

"I really don't know. But I've done a lot of work to learn how to pronounce the guy's name. It's Pre-ZEE-bee."

"And you'd rather not waste that pronunciation effort, I guess. But more importantly, you think it's a good case."

"Well, yes. Medical cases are always suspect, of course, after what the legislature's done with tort reform. But the liability in this case is pretty clear, because of leaving the sponge inside."

"I'll tell you what. I'm much more skeptical. And the reason is, the liability's not perfectly clear, and the damages will be minor. There was infection, yes. And there was lost time and pain, yes. But the incision to recover the sponge was tiny, and they caught the problem right away. Besides, it'll be easy for the defense to provide evidence that cases with left-in sponges are not as rare as you'd think. It sounds really, really negligent, and of course it's not normal, but it happens every day in the big city."

"Okay. But in spite of that, it's negligence, and anyone would decide that."

"Okay. Put Mr. Pre-ZEE-bee in the 'maybe' stack. We'll come back to that one after we see what else we have."

Tom looked at his watch. "It's four thirty. Our jury's going to add another day of no verdict. Unless they come in at five o'clock, as juries so often do."

"Yes. It's not a good sign. With the strength of the evidence that we thought we had, it's not a good sign at all."

* * *

At ten minutes after five, Donna deCarlo buzzed the intercom. "It's Judge Preston's law clerk. Calling for you, Robert."

He held his breath while he answered. "This is Robert Herrick."

"Mr. Herrick, the jury has sent out a note. They're asking Judge Preston a question. The judge wants to get everyone in the case to come to the courtroom as quickly as possible."

"We're on the way."

He walked past Donna deCarlo and said, "Call Randy Westhoven. Tell him to meet us at the courtroom right away. Explain that the jury has sent out a note. Don't go out on a limb trying to tell him anything about the note, and don't speculate. That would be a mistake, because we just don't know what's in it."

* * *

It took just over three hours to get representatives of the parties to the courtroom. It was past eight o'clock when the judge walked up to the bench.

"Good evening, everyone." Judge Pamela Preston smiled. It seemed strange, in these circumstances. "I know you all got here as soon as you could. This isn't going to involve very much decisionmaking on your part, and in a smaller case I probably would have handled it over the phone. But given the length of this trial, I wanted to hear from all of you just in case."

She lifted a piece of paper. "The jurors have sent out a note that asks a question. It is signed by J. P. Samora, the Presiding Juror. Let me just put it up on the screen. Here's what the jury has asked."

Everyone stared. The message gradually appeared on the projector screen, in handwritten letters:

> *If we decide that this blowout was an 'UNAVOIDABLE ACCIDENT,' do we need to answer all of the other questions?—J. P. Samora, Presiding Juror, on behalf of all of the other jurors in this case.*

There was silence. And then there was the loud buzzing of lawyers and clients talking, puzzling, lamenting, and on one side . . . celebrating.

Jimmy Coleman's grin stretched wider than ever. So did the smiles on the faces of the other defense lawyers. And, as they realized what it meant, the smiles worn by the corporate officers grew too.

"What does it mean?" Randy Westhoven asked.

Robert frowned. He felt sick. "It's very bad news. It means that the jurors are leaning toward finding that none of the defendants was negligent."

"I'm inclined not to answer this jury question," said the judge. "I'm inclined to give the jurors the standard non-answer that directs them to do what they're instructed. The old you-are-directed-to fol-low-the-court's-charge-and-instructions answer. Because the instruc-tions already tell them to answer every question."

"Your honor," Robert spoke up. "You should tell them that. I mean, you should tell them to answer each question."

"No, your honor," Jimmy grated. "No, that's not right. The jury is probably hung on most of the questions. It wouldn't do for your honor to order them to answer questions where they can't agree."

"Well, I see there's a difference of opinion." The judge smiled. "Why does that not surprise me? And that's why I'm convinced that a non-answer is what's called for. I'm going to tell them that they're directed to follow the charge and instructions. And that's all."

Robert and Tom left the courtroom in silence, with their eyes fixed on the floor.

41

The hospital administration transferred Pepper Herrick out of the Intensive Care Unit as soon as she was stabilized, within a day of her arriving. "Intensive" care means just that, and it's wasteful to provide it if it's not required.

And the hospital discharged her a day later.

"I hope she'll go to AA," said Robert. Not very hopefully.

"Frankly, I doubt it," said Jonathan.

"Why do you doubt it? She's really been resistant, sure. But this latest thing—acute alcohol poisoning, life-threatening alcohol ingestion—won't that change her mind?"

"Not by the way she's talking."

"Can't you get to her, Jonathan?" Maria wanted to know.

"I can't tell, but I don't think so. Listen, I'm at the end of the road. I'm about to get separated from her. She does this kind of thing too often. I found her just lying on the floor and having spasms or whatever you call them and called 911. I tried to wake her up, but it didn't work. She does it too often."

"Oh. Ohhhh." Robert was speechless.

"When she just gets drunk, she gets mad and destructive toward everyone. I'm afraid for little Robert."

"I know."

"And I'm not sure, but I think by now she's lost her job. Her boss has been pretty good to her. But he's had to know what's going on. The guy isn't stupid and he could see something was wrong and he asked a lot of questions, just as anyone would."

"What can we do?"

Maria echoed it. "What can we do?"

Jonathan's face was pinched. "I don't know."

* * *

On day fifteen of deliberations, the jury sent out another note. Once again, the judge called everyone together.

"The jurors say that they are hopelessly deadlocked," she announced. They say that they can't decide this case. They are asking the court to disband them. In other words, to declare a mistrial."

Judge Preston had the bailiff put the jury's note on the screen. Once again, everyone stared.

> *This jury has worked hard but cannot agree. Everyone is certain that we will never agree. We have voted more than ten times and it always comes out the same. Judge, we seriously ask that you let us out of the jury room. We feel imprisoned.*

The note was signed by "J. P. Samora, Presiding Juror." And it was signed, below Samora's name, by all of the other jurors.

These citizens wanted the judge to know that agreement was hopeless. A verdict was impossible. The jurors couldn't agree, but they all agreed that they would never agree.

Robert and Tom sank in their chairs at counsel table. Jimmy Coleman had a big, dirty grin.

"I'm not ready to dismiss this jury, of course." There was hard determination in Judge Preston's voice. "You all know what comes next. The Allen Charge."

There was a short silence. Then, one of the black suited associates sitting with Jimmy Coleman asked, "What's . . . an Allen Charge?"

The judge either heard the question or anticipated it. "The Allen Charge, as most of you know, is an instruction that we give to juries when they say they are hung. It comes from a case involving a party whose name was Allen, the case where the courts first started approving the charge. It's also called 'the Dynamite Charge,' because it's intended to dynamite loose a verdict. It tells the jurors to keep working and pushes them to reach a decision."

"Your honor, we object," said Jimmy Coleman. "It's too early for that."

"Judge, it's not too early," Robert argued. "It's been fifteen days."

"But it's the first sign of a deadlock," Jimmy protested.

"Well, I think it's time." The judge sounded more than determined. "Bailiff, bring the jury in."

* * *

The jurors were assuming, no doubt, that the judge had heard their message. They shuffled into the courtroom and slowly filed onto the seats in the jury box.

"Mr. Presiding Juror," said Judge Preston, "I have received your note. Let me ask you a question. Without telling me how you are split—or who is for which side—can you tell me what numbers are on each side?"

The Presiding Juror was a too-thoughtful type. The kind of person who weighs everything to an unnecessary degree before answering anything.

There was a long silence, with the Presiding Juror staring upward and seeming to mouth words to himself.

Finally: "It's hard to answer that question because it's fluid, judge. There is a lot of discussion. But I'd say on the next question there are three jurors on one side and the rest on the other."

"All right." Judge Preston's eyes were almost metallic looking in their firmness. "Thank you. Now, ladies and gentlemen, we cannot stop at this point. We just can't. This trial has taken more than six months."

She stared at the jurors one by one. "Please listen, members of the jury, to the instructions I'm about to give you. These are important instructions. Please listen."

Judge Preston held a sheet of paper and read from it:

> *"This trial has been expensive in time, effort, money and emotional strain to both the defense and the plaintiffs. If you should fail to agree upon a verdict, the case will be left open and may have to be tried again. . . . There is no reason to believe that the case can be tried again by either side any better than it has been tried before you. . . .*
>
> *"If a substantial majority of your number are in favor of a given verdict, those of you who disagree should recon-*

sider whether your position is a reasonable one. . . . It is your duty to reach a verdict if you can do so.

"You may be as leisurely in your deliberations as the occasion may require and should take all the time which you may feel is necessary. I will ask now that you retire once again and continue your deliberations. . . ."

The judge added, "I'm giving a written copy of these instructions to the bailiff to provide to you. And Mr. Bailiff, please escort the jurors to the jury room to resume deliberations."

The jurors looked puzzled at first. Slowly, they realized that they weren't going home. They walked slowly behind the bailiff with their eyes cast downward toward the floor.

The same black-suited associate spoke up again. "I see now why it's called the Dynamite Charge."

* * *

"I'm not sure we wanted a Dynamite Charge." Back in his office, Robert was thoughtful and morose. "This is going to make it much more likely that they'll reach a verdict."

"I know." Tom Kennedy nodded. "That earlier note made it pretty clear that they were in a frame of mind to give the win to the defendants."

"We'll file a Motion for New Trial. Which the judge won't grant. She's not about to retry this monster of a case. And we'll file a Motion for Judgment as a Matter of Law, saying that we're entitled to win in spite of the jury verdict."

"Which the judge also won't grant."

"No. She'll say there's evidence on both sides and the jury was entitled to decide in favor of the defendants."

"And then, we'll appeal."

"Which will be subject to what you might call the 'Fat Chance Rule.'"

"Well, yes."

"Nothing to do right now.

"Yeah. That's right. Let's go home.

* * *

The next call from the judge's law clerk came less than twenty-four hours later. "Mr. Herrick, the jurors have announced that they have a verdict."

"We're on our way," he answered. Slowly.

He wasn't eager to hear what the jury had decided.

"No, not now," said the law clerk. "Tomorrow morning at nine o'clock. The hour is late, and the judge is releasing the jury for the night."

"We . . . we are to come to the courtroom tomorrow morning?"

"That's what I just said." The law clerk felt none of Robert's worry. He was just out of law school, and knowing nothing, he thought lawyers had it easy.

Robert called his partner. "Tom, we'll have to get geared up for a night without much sleep."

42

Just after two o'clock in the morning, the man hired by the El Raton cartel—the killer looking for Tom Kennedy—took the elevator to the top floor of the Chase Tower. He found the glass doors locked at the offices of Robert Herrick and Associates.

But he had expected that.

He carried a glass cutter. Not the kind used to slice a pane in a window, but suitable for tearing into a glass sheet two and a half inches thick. Like this set of doors.

This was the address the intruder had for his intended victim. The guy who had sabotaged El Raton's supply chain. That was the *gusano*, the worm, who El Raton thought had justly earned what was about to happen to him.

It took a diagonal cut to make a passageway into the office, because the doors were set into the floor and ceiling. And it took a second cut straight down, because the doors were also anchored into a fixed support in the middle. The intruder slowly lowered the triangular cutout onto the floor and stepped into the office.

The security guard was making rounds. Robert Herrick had been the object of attempted assassinations before, and he believed in security. The guard carried a Glock 22. With fifteen forty-caliber rounds, all more accurate than the intruder's inexpensive Taurus revolver.

The intruder had no idea where to find Tom Kennedy. He had learned that his target was staying here, at this lawyer's office, on a regular basis. He turned to the right, down the hall, to make his search. He walked slowly, because the only light came from the permanent bulbs that were spaced at a distance along the upper walls.

The security guard emerged from the hallway on the other side, at the left, just in time to see a figure slink into the hall across the entry, to the right. This individual carried his weapon in front of him. He was dressed in black and near-black clothes. This wasn't someone who belonged here.

Silently, the guard followed the intruder. The gray-gold carpeting was thick even by the standards of lawyers' offices, because personal injury lawyers need to convey an image of success. Both the intruder and the man who followed him were soundless.

By inches, the guard reached the hallway where the intruder had entered. He kept a distance. Finally, he found what he wanted. A column that held the building intact, and more to the point right now, a column that provided cover.

As a former police officer, the guard knew what to say. He pointed his Glock and shouted, *"Freeze!"* At the academy, so long ago, the sergeant who was the instructor had admitted, "Yeah, friends, it sounds corny." But he had the attention of all of the probationers trying to become police officers when he added, "That's why it works. Everybody knows what it means."

The sergeant had had more to say. "But even if everybody knows what it means, they don't always do it. They may freeze. Or they may not. You have to be ready to shoot if an armed subject turns to shoot you."

By the time they had become full-fledged officers, all of these new recruits had known that you didn't try to shoot an attacker in the arm or knock the gun out of his hand. "That's in the movies," one of their instructors had said. And for that matter, you didn't shoot just to injure an attacker. If you needed to shoot, you needed to shoot to kill.

"Freeze!" was the command, but true to his training, the security guard was ready when the intruder didn't freeze. The man swung his body around, with his Beretta pointed. It was an unwise move, because the guard already had a bead on the intruder, and he ripped off six shots in a row. Quickly.

The intruder fell on his back. The security guard stood still. Shooting with a handgun in relative darkness is notoriously inaccurate. The intruder was bleeding, and he obviously needed help. But that would come later.

"Throw the gun in this direction, where I can see it," the security guard said, again in a loud voice.

The intruder complied this time. The security guard stayed motionless with his G22 pointed. It was impossible to know what other tools of the trade the intruder might have. The guard was calling building security, and he would approach the intruder when he had backup.

There was a sound. Then another sound, and it became clear that it was the sound of a door opening. Tom Kennedy protruded from the space where he lived, in his pajamas. He had a gun too, a Glock 19, which he had obtained on the advice of the security guard.

"Stay there," said the guard loudly. He had no idea whether Tom would make the right moves.

Now, the security guard was dialing another number. "Cop shop," was the answer. "Homicide, Davidson speaking." And the guard gave the officer information that would let him find this location. Building security, he knew, would have immediately called 911 to get radio patrol officers here.

It was only after that that the security guard called 911 to summon an ambulance.

* * *

The morning dawned hot and bright. Robert arrived at the courthouse nearly an hour early. But all that meant was that he waited and worried for a longer time.

Tom Kennedy trudged into the courtroom just before nine. The defense lawyers, including Jimmy's black-suited entourage, were all there.

"Let's just say it was a strange kind of night." Tom rolled his eyes. "And I'll tell you all about it later."

Robert looked at him curiously, but Tom's tone of voice kept him from asking.

Judge Preston ascended to the bench at quarter past nine. "Mr. Bailiff, please bring in the jury." And the courtroom buzzed with impatient speculation.

The jurors filed in, slowly. They looked straight ahead. They didn't turn toward the plaintiffs' table. That was a bad sign, even though they also didn't turn toward the more distant defense table.

"Mr. Presiding Juror, have you reached a verdict?"

"Yes, we have." He sounded weary but satisfied.

"Were you able to answer all of the questions?"

"Yes, we were."

"Please hand the charge and verdict sheets to the bailiff." And everything seemed to float in slow motion, as it always does in this situation, while lawyers, parties, reporters, and spectators all eagerly wait.

The papers went then to the judge, also in slow motion.

The judge studied the verdict. This step would have taken a long time even if it had not been in slow motion, because the jury's answers sprawled over more than a hundred pages of questions.

Finally: "The verdict seems to be in order."

Judge Preston took a deep breath. It was customary, in this area, for the judge to read the questions and answers aloud in front of the lawyers. Even if it was long.

"The first question asks, 'Whose negligence, if any, was a proximate cause of the occurrence in question?'

"And the jury answered, 'Emerald Petroleum Company and Dalliman Services.'"

So far so good, Robert thought. That was the basic issue. But there were many more hurdles to jump. The questions were an obstacle course, and there were many more ways to lose. Especially with the way the jurors had entered the courtroom.

"Next, there is the comparative negligence question, asking what percentages of the negligence found by the jury is attributable to each of the parties."

The judge looked carefully at the verdict. "And the jury answered, 'Sixty percent to Emerald Petroleum Company. Forty percent to Dalliman Services.'"

Tom leaned over and whispered, "The reverse would have been better. But we knew the jury would put more on Emerald because they were the basic cause of the disaster."

"Next," said the judge, "comes the question about whether the employees were all employees of Emerald Petroleum. It asks, 'Were the employees of Dalliman Services and Momex borrowed servants of Emerald Petroleum?'"

Robert and Tom held their breath. A "yes" answer would deny any recovery by anyone against Emerald Petroleum. They noticed that Jimmy looked uncharacteristically anxious too.

"And the jury's answer is, 'No.'"

That was a relief. The jury had found in the plaintiffs' favor on liability.

But that didn't mean that the case was won. There still were the questions about damages. If the jury low-balled the figures here, the plaintiffs would recover, but in small amounts. Jimmy could still win.

"The next question asks, "What sum of money, if paid now in cash, would compensate Randall Westhoven for his damages, if any?"

Again, a breath-holder.

"And the jury answered, 'Twelve million dollars.'"

Robert and Tom stared at the chart that detailed the damages they had requested for each plaintiff. The same chart that was part of the evidence, as Plaintiffs' Exhibit 115.

For Randall Westhoven, the chart said, "Twelve million dollars." In other words, the jury had given them what they'd asked for.

Next the judge read the damages for the death of Lucien Boudreaux. The second plaintiff on the chart. "Eight million dollars," she read. Again, exactly what the plaintiffs' lawyers had asked for.

The rest of the damages came out slowly, as Judge Preston crept through the verdict.

The jury had adopted the figures in Exhibit 115. And it added up to eight hundred million dollars. This must have been a jury that didn't like Jimmy Coleman very much.

The Presiding Juror, J. P. Samora, sat in the front row of the jury box, in the seat nearest to the judge. Robert's eyes met his for an instant, and the Presiding Juror smiled. Robert smiled back.

It had been a bad jury. But now . . . it was a wonderful jury.

Judge Preston finished reading, two hours after she had begun. She put the verdict down on the bench. And said, ". . . Wow."

43

The news media descended on both Robert and Jimmy immediately after the verdict reading ended.

"Mr. Coleman, what comment do you have?"

"Emerald Petroleum is a fine company and the jury's verdict is a terrible mistake."

"Will you appeal?"

"Yes, you bet we will appeal. There are enough reversible errors in this trial to choke a tuna fish."

"Mr. Herrick," said a reporter named William "Whiplash" Gorrick. "Mr. Herrick, are you gonna go kill a fatted hawg to celebrate?"

This newsman was called Whiplash because of his reputation for getting to accident scenes faster than anyone else. And for asking questions that made people jerk their heads backward.

The other reporters laughed, because the question was both interesting and foolish, and they knew Whiplash well enough to know he didn't care.

Tom spoke first. "Whiplash himself might do that, because Whiplash can celebrate having finally stumbled upon what he thinks is a story."

The remark was carefully contrived to make it non-quotable. The man was unlikely to call himself Whiplash on the air, and Tom hadn't said anything newsworthy. The other reporters laughed. So did Whiplash. At least he had a sense of humor.

Robert was more politically correct. "Well, the jury's verdict is a welcome symbol of justice, but there can't be any celebrating. The plaintiffs in this case have enormous losses. They will never recover what the Emerald Rose Disaster has taken from them."

* * *

Trials go on in spite of lawyers' personal difficulties.

Tom told Robert about the intrusion that had happened the night before. There was nothing to do about it now, but there was a need to prevent a similar event in the future.

"Tom, you'd better keep on staying at the office."

"I know." His voice was miserable.

And Robert told Tom about the adventures of Pepper Herrick.

"Robert, won't Pepper come around after this? I mean, surely she'll recognize that there's a problem now, after being hauled to the Intensive Care Unit with alcohol poisoning."

"She doesn't seem to recognize that anything's wrong, at all."

"Every instinct makes me want to give you about five hundred wise suggestions. But I'm sure you've thought of all of them. So I won't."

"Thank you."

"At least we have one thing to celebrate."

"Let's go kill the fatted hawg." Robert laughed. "Not very likely, considering that we have our work cut out for us in the next phases of this case, when Jimmy files his Motion for New Trial and appeals this verdict. And also, considering the problems we have as normal people in addition to the problems we have as lawyers."

* * *

Jimmy Coleman's Motion for New Trial came two days after Judge Preston had signed the judgment in the Case of the Emerald Rose.

It was thirty-seven pages long.

"So that's what those black-suited associates were doing throughout the trial," said Tom.

They each had copies of Jimmy's Motion. They both stopped while reading the second argument.

"Here," said Tom. "This one worries me."

"Me too." Robert frowned.

He read it out loud. "The court should set aside the judgment and verdict, and grant a new trial, because the plaintiffs' expert, Mr. Jonathan Tull, changed his version of the events during trial, and plaintiffs had not updated or supplemented their discovery to notify this defendant, Emerald Petroleum, of the change to Tull's testimony."

Tom read the rest. "And Jimmy claims that the change resulted in a 'devastating surprise' that was so bad that 'defendants were never able to counteract the surprise testimony, even though they would have been able if timely notified.'"

"It's ridiculous, of course." Robert shook his head. "When we answered the written questions at the beginning, Jonathan Tull didn't know the details about the sea water replacement of the drilling mud. We answered with what we knew. And later, when Tull had fuller information, he answered questions in his deposition."

"Yes." Tom's voice was toneless. "But Jimmy claims he didn't know to ask during the deposition about these details, concerning the sea water replacement of the mud, because we didn't update the earlier answers."

Robert frowned. "And technically, we should have updated our answers to the written questions."

"It's a really minor detail, about exactly how much mud there was and how much was left. And it didn't make any difference."

"I know. It's immaterial, and that's our answer. It didn't have to be supplemented or updated because it didn't matter, and even if it should have been updated, it's harmless error because it couldn't possibly have made a difference."

"Well, that's right, of course. But it's a problem, because it's subject to different interpretations. Jimmy knows it didn't make any difference, but he's not about to say so. In fact, he's capable of blowing it up into something really important."

"Yes. And it's an old story. At the time, during the trial, it was supremely *un*important. If we had told Jimmy about it early in the case, he still wouldn't have asked anything about it at trial. But after trial, when the jury's gone and you can't add anything to the witness testimony, the Motion for New Trial looks at it through a magnifying glass. Or rather, through a microscope. And Jimmy blows it up."

"The judge might give Jimmy a new trial."

"And we'd have to try this huge thing another time."

They both stared at the papers that contained the Motion for New Trial.

"Oh, well." Robert sounded upbeat. "The difference didn't matter, and it's really not much of a difference to begin with. And there's one more thing that we've really got going in our favor."

"Which is?"

"Judge Preston sat through this trial. She's not going to want to hear it all again. She'll be aware of what a new trial would mean for her, even if she has to be neutral as to the plaintiffs and defendants. She'll be dead set against a new trial."

But he sounded as though he was trying to convince himself.

* * *

Maybe talking to Rosalie Herrick would resolve his doubts.

"Hi, Mama. . . . Mama Rosalie."

"Hello, Little Robert. It's so nice to see you. What have you been doing?"

"Trying my lawsuit."

"I don't understand."

"I'm a lawyer, remember? And I've been trying a lawsuit."

"I didn't know you were a lawyer. It must be hard work, being a lawyer. And you've been in a trial?"

"Yes."

"I wish there was less of lawsuits in the world. Most of the world wishes there were fewer lawsuits. I don't know who brings them."

He started to say, "I do." But wisely, he didn't.

"I think the best lawyers manage to keep out of the courts. That's what I heard, anyway. Don't the best lawyers stay out of the courts?"

"Yes, Mama. Yes, that's right."

"Aren't there lots of ways to keep out of the courts?"

"Yes. You can settle your cases. In fact, most of them get settled."

"Now, you were saying that you're trying a case. In court, I guess that means. If you get the chance, you should settle that case. You should make it settle."

He looked at her. "Well, if I get the chance, I'll try to do just that."

"Good boy." And she smiled at him.

44

The judge set Jimmy's Motion for New Trial for hearing two weeks after he filed it.

"That's a good sign," Robert said. "She wants to get rid of it."

"Maybe." Tom wasn't so sure.

In fact, neither of them felt comfortable about this hearing.

The day was solid rain. Anyone who crossed the sidewalk to the boxy building that housed the Federal Courthouse got wet, because an umbrella wasn't useful to keep trousers dry.

The courtroom filled with people, exactly as it had during the trial. There were the same lawyers, the same news reporters, and the same spectators. This would be a fun hearing for them, the spectators, because it would involve the same high stakes, but in a compressed time frame.

The judge, true to her habit, walked up to the bench ten minutes late. "Be seated, everyone. We have only one matter on the docket. The defendants' Motions for New Trial in *Westhoven v. Emerald Petroleum Company.*"

She turned to the defendant's table. "Mr. Coleman?"

He stood, as was customary. "Yes, your honor."

"Tell me the arguments that you think are strongest for a new trial. The best arguments in this Motion, that you have in your favor."

"Well, your honor, they're all important, or we wouldn't have listed them. But I'd start with the second paragraph, about the discovery document that Mr. Herrick didn't update."

"That's what I thought you'd say, from the way the Motion is written. Okay. Tell me, just what is the discrepancy you claim existed?"

"The written answers, early in the case, didn't say that the sea water replacement left approximately ten to fifteen percent of the drilling mud in place. Mr. Herrick says that his expert at that time, Mr. Tull, didn't know this. But Mr. Herrick failed to put update and supplement this answer later, when Mr. Tull did know. And for that reason, we didn't know to ask Mr. Tull about it when we took his deposition. But the facts, about ten to fifteen percent of the mud being there, came out as a surprise to us during the trial."

"All right. That's the discrepancy? But your client knew about the ten to fifteen percent of drilling mud, didn't it? Because that fact came from your client in the first place."

"Yes, your honor. But we didn't know that Mr. Tull knew it."

"These facts about the mud came out during the depositions of several others of the plaintiffs' experts, didn't they?"

"Yes, your honor. But we didn't know what Mr. Tull knew."

"You're telling this court, you thought Mr. Tull wouldn't have learned, by the time of trial, what your client knew, and your client's experts knew, and several of the experts on the same side as Mr. Tull also knew?"

"Yes, judge. It was possible he didn't know."

At that, the judge looked like she was on the verge of laughing.

"Well, let me ask you this. Let's go back to the original question, the one that you claim wasn't updated correctly. That question, from you, didn't ask about percentages of drilling mud, did it? It asked, simply, 'Identify and explain all facts, reasons, or factors that you claim had any part in causing the blowout at the Emerald Rose platform.' And the answer provided by Mr. Herrick referred to various causes, including the replacement of mud with sea water, right?"

"Yes, your honor, but they knew we didn't know what Mr. Tull knew. It was their obligation to tell us what he knew."

"But only in response to your questions, right?"

Jimmy hesitated. Then: "Well, yes, your honor."

Judge Preston sat for another hour hearing argument about other parts of the Motion for New Trial. But the questions she asked Jimmy Coleman at the beginning showed how she thought the issues should be resolved.

And her ruling was simple. "The Motion for New Trial is denied. Mr. Herrick, please prepare an order."

As they left the courtroom, Robert said to Tom, "I didn't realize at first what the judge was doing when she first called upon Jimmy Coleman."

"Yes. It wasn't really an argument by Jimmy."

"No. Instead, the judge cross-examined Jimmy. And she showed, pretty firmly, that the so-called error by us didn't make any difference, and in fact it wasn't an error at all."

* * *

"Pepper," said Robert gently, "don't you think it is time for you to go back and actually participate in Alcoholics Anonymous?"

She rolled her eyes. "If it'll do any good, I'll go back to a meeting and sit there. And watch it. But I can't join those people. I can't stand up and swear I'm an alcoholic, because I'm not one."

"Look. You've lost your job because of drinking. You've gone to jail because of drinking. You've lost your weekend service in jail because of drinking. And you've gone to the hospital because of drinking.

"And those are just the recent events. There were lots of earlier events, including your having a wreck and injuring someone because of drinking and having two convictions for driving while intoxicated. Now Jonathan is on the verge of moving out. And he's been loyal to you. What more do you need to convince you?"

"I just know myself, and I know I'm not an alcoholic. I'm just not. I'm not like those people at Alcoholics Anonymous."

"Well, you said just now that you'd go back to AA and sit in on a meeting. That's not what I want. I want you to do more than just sit there. But it's a start. Please go back and visit again."

"Yes, Daddy. But it's not because I need to. It's only because it will make you feel better. I'll do that, because you say you want me to."

"Don't you recognize how many people are worried about you? And even how many people feel hurt because of things you've done?"

"Yes. I'm sorry about having a wreck. I'm sorry about losing my job. But I'll get another one. Those are all occasions when I drank too much. But I don't have to drink too much. And that's what I have decided to do. Not drink as much."

* * *

Whenever Robert got a call from Derrigan Slaughter and Donnie Cashdollar, he knew there was likely trouble coming. These two homicide detectives were like guardian angels.

"But it ain't no problem this time," said Detective Slaughter. "It's good news. That guy in Mexico, whose real name is, ah, Enrico Pedro Nunez Rodriguez y Cavazos—you know, that big bad drug bandit, who they call El Raton—he's in custody. And so is his sidekick named Charro."

"Wow. That is good news."

"Good old Raton, he had his self a girlfriend in town. In Reynoso, Mexico. And the Mexican army shadowed him. You know, they use the army for that, down there. And the army, they knew about how El Raton been goin to this specific place in Reynoso. So they done threw down on him and arrested his sorry ass, right there."

"Not only that," Cashdollar added, "but this guy who broke into your office has been talking, Robert. That was enough to get an extradition warrant on El Raton for attempted murder."

"So Mister Raton, he be outta business. And headed for the good old USA."

"Tom will be happy to hear about this." In fact, Robert thought, Tom will be happy for the first time in a long time.

* * *

The call from Jimmy Coleman came five days after the judge had overruled his Motion for New Trial.

"Robert, my client has a problem. It can pay any judgment. No problem there. But having an unpaid judgment on the books for more than eight hundred million dollars, counting the interest, is something they'd rather avoid. It's a public company, and it affects the stock price."

"I understand." And with that, Robert just waited.

"I've got a potential appeal that we think is a winner. Judge Preston didn't want to retry the case, but the Court of Appeals won't have any reluctance of that kind. They can order it, but they don't have to retry it."

"That's true." Robert waited, still.

"If you are willing to discount the judgment, we can pay it. And your clients will get paid now. A little less, but now."

"Jimmy, what are you proposing to do?" And he waited.

"If you could discount the judgment to five hundred million, we could pay it within ten days."

"I can't recommend that to my clients. It needs to be a whole lot closer to the eight hundred they won. Jimmy, you know that."

"Make it six hundred."

"How about six hundred fifty million, plus all of the interest on the judgment? Which has run up to a significant sum. I could recommend that, I think."

"By that, you mean Emerald's sixty percent share of the judgment."

"I can recommend that."

"Okay. I will get with Emerald and try to get it done. I think, by the way, that Dalliman Services will pay a similar part of its share of the judgment, and I base that on talking to them. I don't know for sure, but I think so."

"Jimmy, I'll have to contact every one of my clients, as you know. Some of them may want to hold out. And endure the appeal, to try to get what they won at trial. But I can recommend this to all of them, and I think most of them will take it. I always think it's best to settle a case if you get fair settlement value for it."

"I know you believe that. But I didn't know whether you'd settle, equally, with a case this size."

"Especially with a case this size. Because big cases can cloud your judgment. Issues that aren't usually important become important in a case this size. You tend to lose your bearings. I think we've avoided doing that on the plaintiff's side, this far. And we should settle if the settlement is the right amount. Especially with a case this size."

*   *   *

After Jimmy said goodbye, Robert sat and looked out the window at the green banks of Buffalo Bayou and the trees of Memorial Park. Then he looked to the south, at the gray, brown and white spires of the city.

He thought about Maria Melendes, because she had told him, "I bet you'll get a call from Jimmy Coleman within a few days. Emerald will be feeling the pressure."

His wife had even said, "And you know, Jimmy will ask you to discount the judgment. And settle the case. And he'll low-ball his first offer, of course. You ought to be ready for him to propose something way under what's realistic. But if you hold on, he'll settle for something like three quarters of the full amount, because Emerald has to get it off the books."

He was glad he had her. She was amazing in so many ways. And besides, he loved her.

He thought about Rosalie Herrick, too. "You should settle that case," she had said. In his life, she was the one with the most wisdom. Alzheimer's? It didn't seem to hold her back. There were so many ways that medicine had discovered, by now, to slow the progress of Alzheimer's Disease.

But then, immediately, he thought about Pepper Herrick.

"It'll never be a perfect world," he whispered to himself. "Too many things have gone right lately. There has to be something that isn't right. And that's my baby. That's Pepper, and it's painful. But I can always look out for her, and I can always hope."

And he thought, "Nothing's ever easy. It doesn't apply only to lawsuits. Nothing important is ever easy in the rest of the world, either, and there, it's not any easier to fix what's not."

———————

Postscript

This book comes as close to reality as a novel can. Or at least, that's been my goal.

But a novel can't mirror real life completely. There are events that are long and boring in real life, and no one wants a novel that is long and boring. For this reason, fiction writers use artificial devices to make their works more interesting than reality. "Dramatic compression," for example, shortens long activities into shorter versions and shoehorns multiple characters into one.

This postscript is intended to tell you what is real in this story and want isn't.

* * *

First, Jimmy Coleman is a kind of caricature. I've never known a lawyer who combined all of Jimmy's unattractive characteristics. He is painted as the ideal villain. On the other hand, I've known lawyers who committed various versions of Jimmy's sins. Some lawyers play it close to the ethical line, and even some who cross it are successful. Some kinds of bad behavior are hard to prevent, and some of the rules are vague enough to encourage exploitation. This isn't a perfect world.

One aspect of Jimmy Coleman that I think is inaccurate is the depiction of his firm, a large firm, as prone to unethical behavior. I don't think big firms are more likely to cheat than small ones. In fact, I think the opposite is true. The worst actors are in the smaller firms or are solo, I'd guess. Maybe the presence of many other successful lawyers projects an expectation of at least minimal adherence to the rules. But the reading public likes a story about a little guy against a big organization and perhaps also conceives of big firms differently from the way I do, and so I've compromised and written it that way.

Does a big-time lawyer like Jimmy, who is defending a suit against an injured plaintiff, really "try the plaintiff?" Yes. All of the psychological literature says that jurors tend to be biased against the victims of accidents. Here's a little story I sometimes tell to law students:

> Bill took a short cut on his way home because he was late for his wife's birthday. He started slowly and cautiously into an intersection. He was T-boned by a drunk driver. Not only did he miss his wife's birthday, but he was seriously injured too.

And the reader's task is to complete the thought, "If only _____."

The typical response is to say, "If only Bill hadn't taken that short cut" or "If only Bill had gone through the intersection faster." But who should be the object of the biggest "If only?" The drunken driver, of course. We ought to be thinking, "If only that guy hadn't driven drunk!"

One reason for this psychological phenomenon is what Jimmy tells Jennifer Lowenstein. People don't want to think of themselves as victims of unpreventable violence. As a result, they tend to think of ways to separate themselves from the victim. Of course, it doesn't always work well for the defendant. It depends on the evidence, thank goodness.

Are lawyers really so amoral as to evaluate good clients by how they pay the bills? Do they think in terms of expo-o-o-sure instead of seeing the immorality of clients who have done something wrong? To a degree, yes. A contrary expectation would ignore the role of the lawyer. In our system, the lawyer is, and is supposed to be, a champion for his client. Of course, the lawyer-champion is supposed to do it all ethically, and it's that, not loyalty to his clients, that condemns Jimmy Coleman. The expectation of our system is that even the most hated, most wretched prisoner has one champion.

I have a friend who practices criminal law who talks about entering the courtroom "with a spring to your step." And what is it that gives you that spring to your step? Is it, perhaps, that your client has a good defense? Or at least something of a defense? No. It's being paid, he says. A lawyer doesn't sit as judge or jury in evaluating his clients.

Like an artisan or an architect, a lawyer has a spring to his step if he is paid for good work. The spring to your step helps you to do a good job.

* * *

The process called "discovery" is accurately shown in this novel, I think. It is costly. Other countries are not so indulgent, and in some places it is even a crime to conduct American-style discovery.

Discovery usually begins with a step that isn't shown here. The parties have to disclose certain kinds of information without being asked. After that, discovery usually involves interrogatories, which are written questions, and requests for documents. The documents may number in the millions with today's electronic media, and just as is shown in this story, there are service companies that will search the millions to tell you which ones to read.

Then, next in order, discovery usually involves depositions: oral questioning of witnesses, which takes place in lawyers' offices, usually. The short excerpts I've shown here are more or less typical of depositions, except that they are little parts of much longer interrogations. The lawyer who takes a deposition has the objective of getting the witness to talk. To run off at the mouth, preferably. Sometimes, a witness who is nervous anyway gets spooked during a deposition and says things that are inaccurate and harmful. And some lawyers are good at precipitating this, just like Jimmy.

Jimmy's Motion to Preserve is an example of the misuse of discovery. Lawyers sometimes use discovery to distract and to balloon the opponent's costs. It's unethical to act for this reason, but the rules don't contain anything specific enough to prevent it completely.

A case like this one would produce millions of documents, just as the story says, and the lawyers would hire search services to parse the documents electronically and identify the documents that matter. It's part art and part science.

The mediation of the case is presented accurately, I think. Different places vary widely about how much they use mediation. In my location, it is practically impossible to obtain a trial setting without first going through mediation. The judges believe in it, and for good reason.

A high percentage of cases settle during or shortly after mediation. The process is nothing more than assisted settlement negotiations, with the mediator as an advocate for settlement and having no power to order anything. But the mediator occupies a neutral role and listens to both parties. An interesting thing happens. Often, people feel as though they have had their day in court, or a loose equivalent of it, after going through a mediation.

* * *

Addition of multiple defendants, as in this case, makes the case more complicated. Plaintiffs often sue multiple defendants in a case like this one. It's a search for guilty parties, as well as parties who can pay.

I've finessed the complexities that would be created by defendants other than Emerald Petroleum—Dalliman Services, Momex, and Amadanko. They would lengthen the trial, and other than occasionally referring to them, I wanted to avoid lengthening the story. The jury charge would be complicated too in a case like this. In fact, the system of comparative liability—who is responsible for what part of the damages—is tremendously complicated in my state, and I suspect in many others.

The jury selection is pictured here as a crucial part of a trial, and it is. The jury studies show that jurors make up their minds early about the types of issues in the case—that is, what the case "is about"—before the evidence begins. The examination of jurors is important for this reason. And also, of course, there is the question of the leanings of the jurors. Give a good lawyer a jury composed of people generally disposed toward the lawyer's case, and victory will usually follow.

Jury selection happens unpredictably. Jurors answer questions in unexpected ways. Sometimes their responses show that they're disqualified. If a lawyer can get that kind of answer, it's like having an extra jury strike. And strange events sometimes happen. I've never seen a potential juror like the crazy man in this story who imagines lawyer conspiracies with senators or thinks all lawyers are Muslim terrorists, but I've seen and heard of strange events.

The most bizarre thing that happened with the jury during one of my trials was that a juror threw up during my closing argument. I was on the ball, so I promptly said, "Your honor, can we have a recess?" After the jury was taken out, the judge, who had a sense of humor, said, "They usually wait 'til he's finished to throw up."

* * *

The preference that Jimmy Coleman has for federal courts, instead of state courts, is typical. Some defense lawyers I know habitually remove every case from state court to federal courts that they can. Although many people don't know it, federal and state courts have a kind of "concurrent jurisdiction," meaning that you can file the case in either court, and if you file in state court the defendant can remove to federal court.

The reasons for the federal-court preference are diffuse. Federal judges each have two law clerks who are recent graduates from the tops of their classes, and this means that the defendant can use more procedural tricks while the plaintiff is just trying to get the case focused and decided. Jimmy's Motion to Preserve, for instance, might have a lesser chance for success in state court. The judge has more control in federal court, and plaintiff's lawyers want the jury to have more power.

And the law that controls the case can be either state or federal law (or a mixture of both). The strange nature of the law in this kind of case—an accident on an offshore platform—is shown accurately in this story. The territory deep offshore is federal, and federal law applies. But the federal government hasn't created a body of law to apply to platforms, and so federal law just "borrows" the law of the upland state. And this way, state law becomes federal law. It's for this reason that the lawsuit can be filed in federal court.

These kinds of issues drive law students (and lawyers) crazy.

* * *

The line of poetry that Robert Herrick quotes is from *The Creation* by James Weldon Johnson. It tells the story of the book of Genesis. Johnson is sometimes identified as one of America's black poets, but he ought to be regarded as one of the world's great poets, period. The entire poem is easy to find online and well worth reading. Here is the beginning:

> AND God stepped out on space,
> And He looked around and said,
> *"I'm lonely—*
> *"I'll make me a world."*

> And far as the eye of God could see
> Darkness covered everything,
> Blacker than a hundred midnights
> Down in a cypress swamp.

* * *

Maria Melendes's case is presented about the way a death penalty case would happen once it got to the federal courts. The case originates in a state trial court, and it goes through the state-court appellate hierarchy, and then the defendant can file a petition for habeas corpus in the federal courts—first at the trial court level, and then in the court of appeals, which is where we see Maria in action. One deviation from reality is that at the federal stage, the prosecution would transfer to the attorney general's office in my state, but it would continue on this way.

The argument about "actual innocence of the death penalty" is real—there actually is such a legal issue.

I know of no case that has held that a properly seized firearm can't be tested without a warrant, and the argument that I dreamed up about that, frankly, seems silly to me. But the Supreme Court case that is the fictional basis for the fictional decision in my story that says there was an illegal search—the case of *United States v. Jones*—is an unusual decision itself, and it seems likely to create all kinds of unpredictable results. The strange decision I thought up for the court of appeals is plausible, if you have strange judges making that decision.

The plea bargaining of Pepper Herrick's intoxicated driving case shows the negotiations about the way I would expect them to occur. I can't claim that the result—the seven-day sentence that is to be served on weekends—is typical, because there isn't a typical sentence for the precise facts here.

Incidentally, plea bargaining has a negative connotation. It shouldn't, any more than settlement of civil cases should, because it's just that: settlement. If we didn't have it, there would be no recognition of the defendant who owns up to his or her fault. We'd need many multiples of the number of prosecutors we have, defense lawyers, judges, clerks, probation officers, and on and on, and the cost would balloon out of sight. And after all, the negotiations are based on predictions of what would happen as the result of a trial. I hope the portrayal of the negotiation process here is more sympathetic than the usual public reaction.

* * *

I don't have much expertise about offshore oil drilling, but Simon Harrall, who is a petroleum engineer, kindly graded my paper. My early draft had a lot of things wrong. For example, I had confused the location and function of the casing. I had excessively downplayed the danger of fires. I had inaccurately described the Blowout Preventers, which usually are a stack of different devices performing different functions, even if they are sometimes referred to as "the" Blowout Preventer, or BOP. And I had made other errors that would have meant that a knowledgeable reader would have seen the story as flawed.

An "annular" Blowout Preventer encircles the wellbore. A "ram" is a different kind of BOP that puts a barrier across the well. A "shear" ram is designed to cut across the wellbore, or shear it. That is, if I have these things right.

I borrowed the causes of the blowout in this story from the Deepwater Horizon disaster. That was the explosion and fire deep in the Gulf that killed eleven people and caused damage to shores in Texas, Louisiana, Missisippi, Alabama, and Florida. It also created a huge lawsuit industry. That disaster, like the one in my novel, involved an inadequate casing, gas leaking, Blowout Preventer failure, an anti-safety culture, and replacement of drilling mud with sea water. That last kind of negligence was a new one on me, but I gather it is done in careful doses for various reasons.

I suspect I still have some things not quite right. And I suspect that the disaster would be unlikely to unfold in the way I've drawn it. The inaccuracies that remain are the responsibility of me, the author, and not of Mr. Harrall. And he warned me that he is not an expert on putting out fires. I guessed that the method I have suggested might have to be modified, because the height of a platform would make it too far away for any manageable boom. It probably would require cutoff below the water.

Dalliman Services, Momex, and Amadanko are contrived to sound like real oil field firms. They are fictional, however, and no real organizations resemble them.

Because my trusted oil patch expert, Simon Harrall, didn't have expertise in oil well firefighting, I had to go elsewhere to get advice about that.

Many years ago, Myron Kinley pioneered the business of fighting oil well fires. He hired Paul Neal "Red" Adair, who became the most famous well firefighter in the world. Red Adair was there to put out the Piper Alpha fire, which is mentioned here as the greatest loss of life in an offshore disaster, and he also fought fires set by Saddam Hussein in Kuwaiti fields after the first Iraqi war. Red Adair is famously quoted as having said, "I've got cut half in two once, and blowed up a time or two, but nothing permanent."

Red Adair had two lieutenants named "Boots" Hansen and "Coots" Matthews. These two separated and formed a firm, which they called Boots & Coots (what else?) Today, Boots & Coots is part of Halliburton, the oil field services giant, but you can still look it up under the old, colorful name. And it's the best known firm for fighting fires today.

So, I called up Boots & Coots. I was fortunate to be switched over to Andy Cuthbert, who is a real bonanza firefighting expert. Andy looked at what I had written in my firefighting scene and saw that I had made the same mistake Robert Herrick makes in my story. I had described the firefighters as putting out the fire with an explosion. Andy politely said he was sorry to lead with this, but "I have some unfortunate news . . . we don't use explosives to put out fires anymore!"

No problem. Andy reworked it, and a few drafts later we had the current version, which puts out the fire the modern way: with a Venturi tube, a jet nozzle shooting sand, and a custom Blowout Preventer. Thanks, Andy!

* * *

Alcoholism is presented in a dramatized way here. It often involves denial, although not always with so much repetition as Pepper Herrick's. The meetings are largely informal, although this story concentrates on the popular conception of typically expected confessions by attendees.

Some of the signs of alcoholism are shown here as they appear in various organizations' literature. The number of signs differs from group to group. Alcoholics Anonymous is the best known of these loose alliances, and its twelve-step program for responding to alcoholism is probably the best known. Some of the steps are mentioned in this story, but there are others among the twelve.

Alzheimer's Disease does bring about the kind of confusion shown here: the failure to recognize people or retain ordinary memories. Sometimes the patient expresses embarrassment. Robert's mother, Rosalie, shares these characteristics, but she also dispenses wisdom that is surprising for her condition. This feature is fictional. I know of no reason to suspect that Alzheimer's patients have any special ability to give out unusually sharp advice.

But I suppose it could happen. And medical advances are gaining on the disease.

* * *

All of my novels have had people asking me about Robert Herrick—about how much he sweats, worries, and feels scared. He's a professional, they say. He would be cool and collected.

But the truth is that many of the best trial lawyers are scared when they begin trials. It's combat, even if without weapons of destruction. It is a battle of presence, of wits, of tactics, of strategy, before the harshest kind of audience: strangers who don't share the combatants' knowledge.

Yes, there are trial lawyers who are fearless, or who seem to be. But many others have to give themselves a pep talk before trying a case. I was one of those.

Just ask a trial lawyer!

— David Crump
2017

Also by David Crump, in the *Robert Herrick Series*

Sudden Death Overtime

The Judas Lawyer

The Target Defendant

Murder in Sugar Land

The Holding Company

Conflict of Interest

Visit us at *www.qpbooks.com.*

www.ingramcontent.com/pod-product-compliance
Lightning Source LLC
Chambersburg PA
CBHW051636260626
47170CB00004B/1203